Trolling
Top To Bottom

Edited by

Mark Romanack

Trolling Top To Bottom

Copyright © 1998 by Mark Romanack
First printing March,1998
Printed in the United States of America

Cover photo by Mark Romanack
Cover design by Turner Seaber Associates
Illustrations by Bill McElroy
Interior layout and design by Kay Richey
Electronically created camera-ready copy by
  KLR Communications, Inc.
  POB 192
  Grawn, MI 49637

Trolling Top To Bottom Edited by Mark Romanack
Fishing / Michigan - North America

ISBN 0-9663017-1-4

799.1   9/3/99   14.95
TRO

Acknowledgments

A book such as Trolling Top to Bottom doesn't come along every day. The combined efforts of some of the finest anglers this sport has to offer, each of the authors of this book deserve recognition and praise. It's a special breed of angler who not only knows his stuff, but who is willing to share the knowledge curve with others. Great anglers are not born, but rather they become successful because of their dedication and commitment to the sport. Special thanks go out to Bruce DeShano, Larry Hartwick, Mike McClelland, Gary Parsons, Keith Kavajecz, Rick LaCourse, Al Lesh, Mark Romanack, Dave Engel, Don Miller, Sam Anderson, Don Parsons, Chuck Cartwright, Bill Sturm and Steve Holt for making this book possible.

The editing skills of Mark Romanack was another vital link in making this project a reality. Mark's close working relationship with the authors of this book made it possible to squeeze every drop of information possible into these pages.

The behind the scenes work of Kay Richey and Bill McElroy also deserves special recognition. Kay's unique talent for designing outdoor books is clearly evident in the professional and attractive look and feel of this book. Bill provided the excellent illustrations that make the information contained on each page easier to understand.

Praise should also be passed along to the masterminds of this project Bruce DeShano and Larry Hartwick of Off Shore Tackle and Riviera Downriggers. Not only are these two tackle manufacturers a couple of talented trollers, they are also among the most successful tournament competitors you'll ever meet. Both these men forged careers in the fishing industry because of their love for the sport and a desire to manufacture quality fishing products.

Off Shore Tackle and Riviera Downriggers are dedicated to producing American made, high quality trolling tackle and accessories. The "Leaders in Trolling Technology", you can trust these companies to bring anglers all the best in trolling equipment.

Dedication

The trolling products produced by Off Shore Tackle and Riviera Downriggers go through many stages of testing before they are released to the public. Behind the scenes countless professional anglers, charter captains and guides test each and every product, suggest refinements, then test again and again.. Ultimately, it's these tireless anglers who make each product the best it can possibly be.

This book is dedicated to those who fish with passion and dedication. Without the support of these professionals, designing, building and delivering quality fishing tackle products would not be possible.

Thanks as always,

Bruce DeShano

Contents

About The Editor

Mark Romanack is a full-time outdoor writer, book author and active member of the Outdoor Writers Association of America since 1988. In the past decade he has penned thousands of national and regional magazine manuscripts, sold countless photographs and authored six books on fishing. An accomplished tournament angler, Romanack spends most of his spare time trolling for walleye, salmon, trout and many other species.

Compiling and editing <u>Trolling Top to Bottom</u> has been a natural extension of Romanack's work. His writing and photography talents have helped make the complex subject of trolling easy for even novice anglers and beginners to understand and enjoy.

For more information on books written by Mark Romanack, check the back of this publication for a complete listing of titles, prices and ordering information.

Introduction

Get ready to troll like you've never trolled before! The information contained in Trolling Top to Bottom can only be described as awesome. More than a dozen of the nation's leading authorities on sport fishing have pooled their knowledge and fishing secrets to create the most comprehensive text ever compiled on the sport of trolling.

Whether you fish for salmon, trout, steelhead, walleye or another species, Trolling Top to Bottom guides you through some of the most effective fishing presentations ever put into print. Inside you'll find chapters jam packed with useful facts about crankbaits, spoons, spinners, in-line boards, catamaran boards, downriggers, bottom bouncers, diving planers, lead core line, snap weights and other trolling hardware. There's also insights into setting up a trolling boat, tips for choosing rods, reels and fishing line, specific tactics for fishing bottom structure, plus little known techniques for trolling up overlooked species such as musky, pike and bass.

With the help of Trolling Top to Bottom, even the most sophisticated trolling presentations become easy to understand and apply. The tactics this book offers can also be applied no matter where you fish, the size boat you own or the species of fish you're most interested in.

Trolling in its many forms is an universal fishing presentation that works everywhere and for almost everything that swims. In fact, some of the trolling techniques outlined in this book have been outlawed on select waters and for certain species. No kidding! Trolling is such an effective way to catch some species that special regulations are often needed to prevent anglers from overharvesting the resource.

The fastest route to a limit of fish is a trolled line. Read on and get ready to enjoy a whole new caliber of fishing with your family and friends. Soon you'll be trolling like you never trolled before and catching fish you never dreamed possible.

Best fishes,

Mark Romanack

Mark Romanack, Project Editor

Chapter 1
Why Trolling?
By
Bruce DeShano

Fishing isn't a hobby or a pastime for the authors of this book, it's their livelihood. A tournament fisherman, guide or charter captain's job is to bring fish (the bigger the better) to the dock, then share the techniques that made the catch possible with all who will listen. Promoting fishing is what these professional anglers are all about.

Even a novice angler would have to be pretty dense not to have noticed how trolling in its many forms has dominated much of the fishing scene in recent years. There's not a direction you can point to or a fishery you can mention that doesn't have the potential to produce a trolling bite. Walleye, bass, salmon, trout, stripers and even panfish fall prey to trolling tactics.

Even in the heartlands of North Dakota, South Dakota, Wisconsin and Minnesota where trolling has no foot hold in tradition, long time "jiggers and live bait riggers" have recognized how beneficial trolling can be and are changing the way they fish. So why are guides, tournament pros and recreational anglers trolling more these days? The answer to that question can be summed up in one word "efficiency".

Trolling is an efficient means of fishing multiple lines and presenting a wide assortment of lures at varied trolling speeds. In short, trolling brings a lot of positive virtues to the party.

The ability to quickly cover water when searching for fish is one of the greatest assets of trolling. Fishing is largely a process of eliminating unproductive water. Trolling, by its very nature eliminates water more quickly that traditional techniques including casting, drifting or rigging.

Once fish are located, trolling allows the angler to present multiple

11

The typical trolling boat looks like a porcupine when all the rods are set. The ability to fish using multiple lines is one of the major reasons trolling is more productive than other forms of fishing.

lines at precise depth levels. Think about it, isn't fishing two or more lines better than one? You bet, especially when fishing is tough and the angler needs every possible edge.

Trolling is also a mechanical skill that's easily taught to and shared with other fishermen. The variables of a successful trolling pattern are tangible. Lure model and color, trolling speed, lead length, lure running depth, water depth; all of these variables and more are easily communicated and shared with other anglers.

In fact, trolling is one of the few angling methods that make it easy for families to get kids hooked on fishing. Imagine trying to teach a newcomer the skills of casting and retrieving a jig. Chances are the desire the novice has to learn will be long gone before the first fish bites.

Many families make the trolling experience more fun and educational

There are a lot of reasons to troll, but this style of fishing ranks as one of the best ways to introduce kids and novice anglers to sport fishing. In a trolling situation it's easy to share the fun and excitement with others.

by letting the kids participate in the lure selection and line setting process. When a fish is hooked, not only does a child have fun reeling it in, but there's a sense of satisfaction in knowing the new angler was involved in the fishing process.

While you're waiting for the first bite, let the kids enjoy a snack, some drinks or even a video game. Try that trick while working a jig or live bait rig!

Also, we would be remiss if we didn't report that trolling routinely produces larger fish than other fishing methods. A quick check with any master angler program will prove that most record size fish are taken using one of many different trolling techniques.

Perhaps it's the fact that trolling keeps the lures in the strike zone 100% of the time or that trolled lures simply cover more water, but there's no disputing reality. Trolling simply produces bigger fish per angling hour than any other fishing method.

Combine these facts with the realization that the newest and hottest fishing techniques are trolled presentations, and it becomes easier to see why anglers are embracing trolling in its many forms.

Trollers depend on a different set of "tools" when fishing than the typical angler. When it comes to trolling tools, Off Shore Tackle and Riviera Downriggers are industry leaders. Manufacturers of pinch pad style planer board releases, downrigger and stacker releases, manual and electric downriggers, double board skis, planer masts, in-line boards, trolling weights and a host of other products that help anglers maximize their fishing efficiency.

Trolling Top to Bottom is the most comprehensive book ever compiled on the subject of trolling. Contained within the following pages are the angling secrets of the leading walleye, bass, salmon, trout and striper anglers this nation has to offer. Each chapter is authored by a different tournament professional, guide, charter captain or outdoor writer. These anglers have made sport fishing their life work, not just a weekend hobby.

Collectively, this book represents thousands of hours of one-the-water experience. Covered in detail are the basics of trolling, plus the latest techniques and tricks that can help transform an average day on the water into memories that will last a lifetime.

If you enjoy catching big fish like this monster brown trout, trolling is the way to go. Dale Voice caught this 34 pound 4 ounce brown trolling a Storm ThunderStick behind a Side-Planer board.

15

No topic has been overlooked. In the pages that follow you'll find detailed information dealing with the tools of the trade including downriggers, diving planers, in-line boards, catamaran boards, in-line weights, bottom bouncers, crankbaits, spoons, spinners, lead core line, and wire line. In addition there are chapters aimed specifically at bass, walleye, salmon, trout, striper and night fishing tactics.

Trolling Top to Bottom also features a wealth of photographs and illustrations that help make the message as clear as possible. After all, the goal of this book is to make trolling a part of every angler's mind set.

So when anglers ask why you're trolling, simply smile and report that the shortest distance between the dock and a limit is a trolled line!

In the next chapter we'll attack the problem of setting up a boat for trolling. Whether you own a 12 foot car-topper or a 30 foot cruiser, just about any boat can be converted into a trolling machine.

Bruce DeShano is the CEO of Off Shore Tackle Company and innovator of trolling accessories.

Chapter 2

Setting Up A Trolling Boat
By
Mark Romanack

Have you ever noticed how a teenage boy primps, polishes and putters with his first car? The ride might be a rust bucket to you and me, but to that kid a car represents freedom, a chance to be independent, in control and making decisions.

That's the way I feel about every fishing boat I've owned. My fishing boats are a ticket out of the office and into a world without deadlines. To date I've owned 13 walleye boats. Rigging each one has been a labor of love and an on going extension of the sport I enjoy so much.

I've yet to meet a angler who didn't feel the same way. Most anglers enjoy custom rigging a fishing boat almost as much as the line wetting process. After all, it's the selecting and mounting of essential accessories that transforms an ordinary boat into a floating fish trap.

The interesting thing is no matter how much you putter around selecting and mounting kicker motors, electronics, rod holders and other essential fishing tools, there are always improvements that can be made.

After rigging 13 boats I'm living proof of this fact. Every new boat I rig receives new equipment and improvements. Some of the changes are as subtle as moving a rod holder so it functions better and others are profound as adding an auto-pilot or differential GPS module.

When a boat is rigged properly, not only does it perform and function at its best, it makes the fishing experience much more enjoyable.

A WORD ON BOATS

The suggestion that there's a perfect trolling boat is a myth. The sport of trolling is so broad based that there could never be just one boat

The concept of the all purpose trolling boat is a myth. No single boat can meet all the trolling requirements anglers are likely to encounter. On big water large boats like this 27 foot SportCraft or 23 foot Pro Line (facing page) are good choices.

ideal for every trolling situation.

When fishing big bodies of water like the Great Lakes, 21 to 30 foot boats are a logical choice. Most boats in this class feature a cutty cabin or other enclosure that affords some protection from the elements.

Mid-sized boats in the 17 to 20 foot class are a good choice for inland waters or fishing on the Great Lakes during reasonable conditions. In recent years many boats in this class have become known as "walleye" boats. Built by over two dozen different manufacturers, these boats are good examples of a mid-sized craft that can be used to troll for a wide variety of species.

There's also need for smaller trolling boats. Some outstanding fishing opportunities take place on remote waters where the luxury of a paved boat launch doesn't exist. A 12 to 16 foot aluminum boat or even a square stern canoe can be converted into an excellent troller.

The problem with boats is no matter which one you buy, you'll never be completely satisfied. Perhaps that's a good thing? With so many excellent boats to choose from and so many trolling situations to explore, it could take years of sampling different models to find a boat that's ideal for your style of fishing. My advice is that while you're searching for that perfect boat, enjoy the ride!

BASIC AS BATTERIES

Many anglers don't think much about the batteries in their fishing boat. Big mistake. Just about everything in a fishing boat depends on battery power. You need battery power to start the engine, run sonar units, electric motors, bilge pumps, livewell pumps, navigation lights, the VHF radio and more.

The most important battery in a fishing boat is the cranking battery. Marinas rig fishing boats with a starting battery that features 500 to 600 cold cranking amps of power. A power source this size is adequate to crank over a large V6 outboard, but when you add up the amp draw from all the other accessories this battery must run, it's easy to see that 600 amps isn't adequate. A livewell pump alone can draw enough amps during the course of a day to leave one of these average batteries lifeless.

The best option is to start with a heavy duty marine/RV battery that features 1000 cold cranking amps. The extra power is just what you need

20

Mid-sized boats like this 18 foot Champion Fishunter fill an important niche in the trolling scene, but there's also need for small boats (below like this aluminum model used to troll up a back country lake trout.

for running the multitude of accessories on a boat and still having enough juice to crank over the big engine when it's time to head for home.

When you purchase a heavy duty battery, be sure to buy a battery tray and tie down straps. Chances are this large battery won't fit in the battery tray that came with your boat.

Deep cycle batteries are required to run an electric motor. Small boats can usually get by nicely with a 12 volt system, but anything 17 foot or larger is going to require the power of a 24 volt system.

I feel the same way about deep cycle batteries as I do about cranking batteries. You can't have too much power. Buy the highest amp batteries you can find and you'll avoid a lot of headaches down the road.

Good batteries don't come cheap. Expect to pay $80.00 to $125.00 each for a quality battery. High amp batteries cost a lot more, but they also come with an extended warranty that makes them the best possible investment.

Batteries are heavy and care must be given to insure they are mounted securely to the boat floor. It's also important to mount batteries in places that are easy to get to for charging and maintenance.

The batteries in your boat need frequent care and maintenance if they are to provide dependable power. You should get in the habit of charging deep cycle batteries after every trip and it doesn't hurt to put a charge into your cranking battery from time to time, especially after trips that used a lot of accessory power.

The easiest way to charge batteries is with a built-in charging system. Chargers are available that charge two deep cycles or two deep cycles and a cranking battery at the same time.

If you don't own a built-in charging system a simple 10/2 amp portable charger will get the job done one battery at a time. Most portable chargers feature a 10 amp setting for deep cycle batteries and a two amp setting for cranking batteries.

At the end of the fishing season, make sure all batteries are fully charged and removed from the boat. Store the batteries in a cool place where they are out of the way. If the batteries are stored on a cement floor, be sure to place pieces of wood between the batteries and the con-

Not long ago a Loran-C unit was a common sight on a trolling boat. Today Global Positioning Systems (GPS) use signals from a series of satellites orbiting the Earth to provide more accurate and dependable navigation data.

crete floor. A battery left on a cement floor will be slowly zapped of power. Eventually the unit won't even take a charge.

ELECTRONICS

A quality sonar unit, a GPS navigation system and a dependable marine radio are three pieces of electronic equipment I recommend be mounted on every fishing boat. In the case of some models both sonar and GPS navigation are combined into the same unit. These popular units have become the standard all other sonar/GPS units are compared to. Purchasing a combined system is more economical and it also saves valuable space on the console for a compass or another electronic aid.

A GPS/sonar unit should be mounted in a position to be used as the primary sonar unit. On console boats I'd recommend mounting this unit on the driver's console. In tiller boats I'd suggest mounting the unit on the port side near the back of the boat. Many tiller boats feature an electronics box that's designed to give expensive sonar a little extra protection and security.

Instead of bolting or screwing a sonar/GPS unit permanently, I'd suggest using a Johnny Ray quick disconnect bracket. Quick disconnect brackets (I suggest purchasing and using the largest size) allow the unit to be easily removed for storage or to be mounted in a different location. All that's needed to mount a sonar unit for use in the bow or another area of the boat is an extra Johnny Ray base, power cord and transducer.

The power cords on sonar and GPS units should be wired directly to the battery with a fuse harness mounted near the sonar unit. These critical pieces of fishing equipment are often wired to an accessory switch on the console. Wiring a sonar unit or other electronic aid to an accessory switch is adding another link in the system that can fail.

Keep it simple when wiring electronics. When problems arise, and they will, tracing down and making repairs will be easier.

A VHF radio should be mounted so that the antenna cable is routed away from sonar power leads and transducers. I normally run the VHF antenna on one side of the boat and sonar transducers, GPS cables, etc., down the other side of the boat to avoid electrical interference.

The radio itself should be mounted where it receives some protection from rain or spray. Even units that are advertised to be waterproof

24

fair best when they are protected from the elements.

If the radio is mounted underneath the console it may be necessary to wire an auxiliary speaker so the radio can be easily heard. If you choose to add an auxiliary speaker make sure to purchase a marine grade model. A normal car speaker will short out and be useless the first time it gets splashed or rained on.

ROD HOLDERS

Something as simple as a rod holder should be a snap to mount. Unfortunately, rod holders aren't as easy to mount as you might expect. These invaluable fishing aids always seem to end up in spots that interfere with other equipment such as swivel seats and livewell lids or in spots that impede the function of the rod holder itself.

A lot of the problems associated with rod holders stem from poorly designed products. For every quality and functional rod holder on the market there are half a dozen worthless models.

Quality nylon rod holders such as the Fish On models produced by Tempress can be mounted on any boat and cost around $20.00 each. Stainless steel tube style holders produced by Tite Lok and other companies run up to $40.00 each. Considering that a fishing boat will need from four to 10 rod holders, it's easy to see why anglers are sometimes swayed into shopping for bargains when it comes to these accessories.

The problem is what looks like a bargain ends up costing the angler more money in the long run. Bargain rod holders break when you need them most. More than once I've seen a $100.00 line counter reel lost overboard when a rod holder failed at the worst possible moment.

I purchase quality Fish On and Tite Lok rod holders for all my boats. When I sell a boat, I list the rod holders as accessories and place a price tag on them. In some cases the customer chooses not to purchase the rod holders, so I simply remove them and mount them on my next boat.

I personally favor the rail mount versions that allow me to mount my rod holders without drilling holes in the boat. Al Lesh, a charter captain and tournament angler from the Detroit area uses an unique rod holder system on his Lunds.

Al bolts a piece of hardwood approximately 2 inches wide, by three inches tall, by 36 inches long onto the flat gunwale of his boat using two stainless steel bolts. Onto this piece of hardwood Al screws into position four Fish On side mount adapters. Each adapter accepts an adjustable Fish On rod holder allowing Al to fish up to four rods per side. Al's design only requires two holes to be drilled in the boat per side and can be easily removed and mounted to another boat when it's time to buy and sell.

The best advice I can give regarding the mounting of rod holders is to take it slow. Sit in the boat and imagine how you'll be fishing and where the most convenient locations for rod holders will be. Before you drill the first hole, make absolutely sure the rod holder will be able to swivel and tilt properly. Also, take a second to note that the rod holder doesn't interfere with seats, rod boxes or livewell lids. Once you've drilled the holes, you'll have to live with your decision.

KICKER MOTORS/TROLLING PLATES

Serious trollers use one of two accessories to control boat speed. A small gasoline kicker motor or a trolling plate mounted on the main outboard or I/O is the only practical way to go when it's important to troll at slow, normal and fast speeds. Trolling with the main outboard or I/O works fine at speeds from 2-4 mph, but most of these products simply won't idle down slow enough to fish spinners, wobble glows, dodgers and many other slow trolling presentations.

A kicker motor is a work horse when it comes to trolling chores. For most fishing boats a 10 or 15 horsepower model is an excellent choice. Kicker motors may be mounted on the transom or a bracket that attaches to the back of the boat.

Most of the brackets designed to handle kicker motors operate manually, but a few models raise and lower the motor with an electric or hydraulic pump that works much like the power trim on an outboard motor. Electric or hydraulic kicker motor brackets cost between $500.00 and $1000.00, but they also provide valuable protection for the kicker when running in rough water.

More than a few kickers have become insurance statistics when the bracket broke while running in rough water and the motor went for a swim. To avoid damaging the kicker many anglers tilt their engine into

26

the upright position then use a ratchet strap to secure it so the motor doesn't bounce when running. Strapping the motor every time you move from spot to spot is an inconvenience, but it's the best way to avoid damage to this critical piece of trolling equipment.

A trolling plate is another way to control boat speed. Frankly, most of the trolling plates on the market are band-aids that only do a fair job of slowing down the boat. Many are made from thin steel that's destroyed the first time you forget to raise the trolling plate and put the boat up on plane.

Riviera Downriggers produces an electric trolling plate known as the PTC which stands for Perfect Trolling Control. The trolling plate attaches to the cavitation plate of outboards and I/O units and uses a powerful electric motor that moves a cast iron plate up or down. The unit has a momentary switch that allows the plate to be positioned anywhere from all the way up to all the way down. By simply tweeking the switch the trolling speed can easily be adjusted from .5 to four MPH.

The greatest advantage of the PTC is it allows boat speed can be managed while allowing your engine to run at a little higher RPM level. Keeping the main engine running a little faster helps to reduce problems with fouled plugs and carbon choked carburetors. For more information on the PTC call Riviera at 1-517-738-5600.

AUTO-PILOTS

Once you've purchased and mounted the basic trolling essentials, you may want to spend a little more cash and see how an auto-pilot can make fishing easier and more enjoyable. Most auto-pilots are gear driven devices that control the boat by moving the steering cable or by attaching directly to the outdrive of the boat. A small margin of error is involved in these auto-pilots, because of differences in the adjustment or natural wear of steering systems. Still, most auto-pilots will keep the boat moving on course with only a few degrees of fudge factor.

A second type of auto-pilot mounts directly to a kicker motor and uses a small hydraulic pump and electronic compass to sense and control boat movements. The TR-1 Auto-Pilot is the only unit on the market designed to be used with kicker motors from six to 25 horsepower.

Like other auto-pilots the TR-1 can be interfaced with a Loran-C or

GPS unit making it possible to navigate to a known point on the water. The unit also has a hand control that allows changes in course to be made by simply rotating a switch.

For owners of four stroke kickers there's also a remote control that allows both engine speed and direction to be managed from one control. This unique product runs around $1500.00 and can be installed in about two hours if you're handy with some basic tools.

A third type of auto-pilot is an electric motor that has the ability to actually follow bottom contours! The Pinpoint electric motor combines sonar and computer technology into a unit that senses bottom depth and makes staying on a breakline or weed edge easy.

In a practical fishing situation this is how the Pinpoint works. Imagine positioning your boat along a break, then setting the electric motor to keep the boat in that depth range. Adjust the trolling speed to suit the needs of your chosen fishing presentation and then go fishing.

The Pinpoint will sense changes in the bottom depth and keep the boat moving along the break like a beagle following a rabbit track. The angler is free to fish with two hands making it much easier to fish a second line or to change baits, etc., meanwhile the boat stays on course.

The Pinpoint is currently available in a 24 volt model designed for full sized bass and walleye boats. Eventually I'd expect to see this product available in a smaller and less expensive unit for the owners of modest aluminum boats.

These are just some of the accessories you can mount to a fishing boat that make our sport more productive and enjoyable. The list of accessories (toys) is never ending and so is the process of boat rigging. No matter how much time you spend rigging and rerigging, there's always going to be new accessories or better ways to mount them.

If you're like me you simply keep buying and mounting accessories until there's no room left for more. Then you go out and buy a bigger boat and start the process all over again!

Our next chapter focuses on the subject of rods, reels and fishing line. A serious troller takes great pride in his or her equipment and makes sure these items are matched and balanced.

Chapter 3

Trolling Rods, Reels & Lines
By
Mark Romanack

I can tell instantly when anglers are rookies at the art and science of trolling. I look at their rods, reels and fishing line. If these basic pieces of fishing equipment don't match and the reels are half filled with obviously different types of fishing line, my fears that I'm dealing with non-believers are confirmed.

If I had a nickel for every time I've seen someone trying to troll with equipment intended for completely different fishing applications, I'd be on my way to replace the worn collection of trolling rods and reels I've trusted for over 15 years.

Despite what you may have heard or read, trolling is actually a simple method of fishing. The rules of the game are flexible, with one major exception. No matter what trolling method is being used, when fish are located and caught, the next step is to duplicate that technique as exactly as possible with other lines. That means selecting more lures of the same model and color, duplicating the trolling lead, matching the boat speed and even making sure the pound test line used is identical.

These variables are what make or break a trolling presentation. It's obvious why it's important to select other lures of the same model and color, but a lot of anglers simply don't understand why the other variables are just as important.

Duplicating the trolling lead insures that additional lines and new baits will fish at the same depth range that originally produced fish. Lead length can have a profound impact on lure diving depth and in some cases lure action. This is true when fishing crankbaits and spoons.

Trolling speed is another misunderstood trolling variable. The speed

29

A classic trolling combination, this Shakespeare Ugly Stick and Daiwa 27 LC line counter reel has seen lots of use. Note how the paint has worn off the wooden handle. Had this rod been equipped with a cork hankle, it would have needed replacing years ago.

a lure moves through the water influences action. Even a slight change in speed can destroy a lure's strike triggering action. That's why anglers often catch fish trolling in one direction, then when they turn around to go through the school again they don't catch anything. What usually happens is when the boat turns around the speed changes. Even slight changes in speed caused by trolling into or against the wind can make a big difference in how fish react to trolled lures.

Line diameter is something many anglers don't think much about, but they should. The diameter of fishing line plays a big part in how deep lures will run. Thinner lines allow lures to fish deeper, while lines that are larger in diameter produce more drag in the water and force lures to run closer to the surface. The difference in lure running depth between 10 and 17 pound test can be several feet. More than enough to influence how fish react to passing lures.

Each of these trolling variables has been detailed to make an important point. The ability to accurately duplicate a productive presentation is the foundation all good fishing is based on. This fact is precisely why trollers often catch more fish than anglers using other methods. With trolling it's fairly easy to reproduce a productive technique using other lines, so long as some attention to detail is taken.

With these facts in mind, take my word for it when I say that there's no way to accurately duplicate productive trolling techniques if the rods, reels and lines used are not matched and balanced. You can cut a lot of corners in fishing and get away with it, but when it comes to trolling you can't get by without a matching set of rods and reels all loaded with the same pound test line.

When trolling for walleye, bass and other medium sized species I recommend spooling up with 10 or 12 pound test line. For larger fish such as salmon or steelhead you'll need lines in the order of 17 pound test.

Those of you who troll for many different species have two options. Either you purchase two sets of trolling rods/reels equipped respectively with the ideal line sizes or you'll have to settle for one set of rods and reels and simply switch lines as needed.

Luckily most trolling applications can be handled with a downrigger style rod and line counter reel. Two exceptions to this rule come to mind.

Dipsy Divers are large diving planes that have a tremendous amount of drag in the water. A stout rod designed especially for using these divers is needed for serious Dipsy fishing. Normally Dipsy rods are nine to 10 feet long with a heavy action and strong backbone. The ideal reel for this rod would be a Daiwa SG47LC line counter reel equipped with 20 to 30 pound test monofilament.

Also, any technique that requires the angler to hold the rod while fishing, calls for triggersticks similar to those commonly used for bass fishing. Usually made of high modulus graphite and equipped with a baitcasting style reel, this rod and reel combination should be six-and-a-half to seven feet long and feature a medium action. A rod and reel of this caliber is handy when flatline trolling with bottom bouncers, crankbaits or three way rigs.

For general trolling with downriggers, planer boards, and Snap Weights I favor a downrigger style rod around eight feet long. The best rods are those made of fiberglass or a graphite/fiberglass composite with an action rating for 10-20 pound test line. These rods should be equipped with a foam, not cork handle. Cork simply can't take the abuse of being slid in and out of a rod holder constantly.

I also look for rods that feature a slow action that spreads out the strain of fighting big fish throughout the rod blank. A good trolling rod should act like a shock absorber for the fishing line. If the rod features too fast an action, the tip section of the rod ends up handling all the strain and often ends up breaking.

My reel choice and the choice of most serious trollers is the Daiwa SG27LC line counter reel. Brand loyalty aside, this is the only quality reel on the market that features adequate line capacity, a dependable star drag, a bait clicker and a line counter that is accurate, dependable and measured in feet.

The bad news is one of price. These quality reels aren't cheap, starting at around $100.00 each. Competitive reels on the market are priced to sell, but my experience with these products hasn't been good. Considering that the SG27LC reels I currently own have given me faithful service for over 15 years I have no grounds to complain about the price.

For general trolling with downriggers, planer boards or flatline applications it's tough to beat a downrigger style rod like this Quantum XL series matched with a line counter reel.

33

If line counter reels are just too expensive for your budget, I'd suggest one of the many quality level wind reels on the market. Quantum, Daiwa, Penn, Shimano and Abu Garcia all manufacture excellent trolling reels in sizes similar to the SG27LC. Quality levelwind reels start at about $50.00 each. Unfortunately these reels don't featured a digital line counter, but there are other ways of measuring trolling leads.

If your reel of choice doesn't feature a line counter, I'd suggest one of several techniques for metering trolling leads. One of the easiest techniques is to purchase a fishing line that's marked at specific lengths. Metered fishing line works great, but it's tough to find. Many anglers simply measure and mark their own line using a felt tipped pen.

Another method of measuring lead lengths is known as counting bars. When letting line out, simply count how many times the line passes back and forth across the face of the spool. This crude method of measuring lead length is amazingly accurate so long as every reel is the same size and model. Also each reel must be filled with exactly the same amount of line and the line needs to be the same pound test.

Many anglers monitor leads by simply grasping the line near the reel and pulling off one arm length at a time. This method works, but what if your arms are longer or shorter than a fishing buddy? It's easy to see why line counter reels are so popular with serious trollers.

Also, avoid line counter devices that mount on the rod. None of the add-on line counters I've tested can be trusted.

A downrigger rod equipped with a SG27LC handles 80 to 90 percent of my trolling needs including walleye, brown trout, salmon, steelhead, pike and even musky fishing. The specialty rods and reels outlined earlier in this chapter are worth investing in if you plan on using these angling methods. My advice is to add these rods and reels to your equipment list as you need them.

TROLLING LINES

A good trolling line and a good casting line are two different animals. The properties that make for a good trolling line, are a casters nightmare. Trolling lines need to feature low stretch, high abrasion resistance, excellent knot strength and toughness. Good trolling lines are stiff and they tend to have a lot of memory.

When it's necessary to hand hold a trolling rod, triggersticks like this one are good trolling rods. Triggersticks can even be used for light trolling duties such as walleye fishing with in-line boards, but these rods are too light for downrigger fishing and many other trolling applications.

In comparison, a good casting line should be limp, soft and feature low memory or coil when it comes off the spool. When casting lines are used in trolling situations it doesn't take long for disaster to occur. The soft texture of casting lines simply can't stand up to the abrasion and line abuse trolling often dishes out. More fish than I care to comment on have been needlessly lost because the angler spooled up with a casting line instead of a heavy duty trolling line.

When selecting a monofilament line for trolling, read the package to see what features the line offers. Words like limp or castability suggest the product is designed for casting. If abrasion resistance or low stretch are the key features, you've found a trolling line.

All the major line manufacturers produce monofilaments specifically designed for trolling situations. The brand you choose is a personal decision, but make sure the line is of premium quality. Premium lines feature quality control standards that insure uniform diameter and break strength throughout. Discount lines like those sold in department stores aren't subjected to these high standards.

Before rushing to save a buck or two on a spool of no name line, remember what's responsible for linking the angler and fish together.

Even quality fishing line wears out and must be replaced. I'd suggest replacing your line at least twice a year and more if you fish frequently in areas that feature submerged rocks, wood and other debris.

SPECIALTY LINES

These days there are lots of specialty lines on the market designed for specific purposes. Some of these lines feature low stretch, while others are known for super high abrasion resistance. Lines that feature low stretch can be especially useful for many trolling situations. Normal monofilament stretches like a rubber band when wet, making it more difficult to get solid hooksets.

Stren's new Sensor line has 50% less stretch than other monofilament lines without giving up knot strength or abrasion resistance. Because Sensor is a monofilament line, it works well in the pinch pad releases commonly used with in-line boards, trolling weights, downrigger and stacker releases.

Anglers interested in high abrasion resistance will find that Silver Thread's Excalibur is one of the toughest lines on the market. This line has amazing abrasion resistance, making it an excellent choice when trolling in situations where the line is sure to come in contact with submerged rocks, wood and other debris.

The newest generation of braided lines are also catching a lot of attention. Most of these products are manufactured from two different fibers known as Micro Dyneema and Spectra. These super tough and thin fibers allow for lines with near zero stretch and amazingly thin diameters.

While many anglers swear by the super braids, a lot of trollers swear at them. These lines have two primary problems. First off, super braids are very expensive. It can easily cost $20.00 or more to spool each reel with a super braid. Secondly, the ultra low stretch of these lines makes it easy to over-fight fish and lose fish.

Despite these drawbacks, super braid lines do have some important trolling applications. Whenever it's important to achieve maximum crankbait diving depth, super braids are a logical choice. Because these lines are so thin, it's possible to achieve up to 50% greater depth diving ability when fishing braided line compared to comparable break strength monofilaments.

Super braids are also finding a home with those who enjoy trolling Dipsy Divers. The low stretch characteristics of super braid makes it easy to trip divers when it's time to change locations or lures. Also, the thin nature of super braids allows divers to reach much greater depths than possible with monofilament.

Anglers who choose to use super braids should use some common sense precautions. A slightly softer rod action than normally used is a good idea when fishing super braids. Also, be sure to set the reel drag a little lighter than normal and take it easy when fighting fish. If these precautions are taken, most of the problems associated with braided lines can be avoided.

The rods, reels and fishing lines selected for trolling are essential pieces of fishing equipment. If you're just learning the trolling game, do yourself a favor and buy matched and balanced equipment from the start. If you already own a bunch of odds and ends, hold a garage sale and soon. Remember, the secret to trolling success is the ability to reproduce effective presentations with other lines. Don't fool yourself into thinking you can accomplish this task with mis-matched rods, reels and line.

With the topic of rods, reels and line mastered, it's time to move on to the popular subject of crankbait trolling.

Chapter 4

Precision Trolling Crankbaits
By
Bruce DeShano

All crankbait trollers have one thing in common. They need to know how deep their favorite lures dive.

Depth control is everything when trolling crankbaits. It doesn't take a rocket scientist to figure out that crankbaits won't catch walleyes, pike, trout, salmon and other species unless the lures are presented close to waiting fish.

Little information on lure diving depth was available until recent years. Even most crankbait manufacturers didn't know how deep their lures would run.

It wasn't until 1989 that noted walleye pro Mike McClelland stunned the tackle world when he introduced his book Crankbaits. A guide to trolling and casting depths of over 200 crankbaits, McClelland's trolling data soon proved to be a bench mark for anyone who fishes crankbaits.

All of McClelland's trolling data was based on lures fished at or near their maximum diving depth. A trolling lead of 120 feet was chosen by McClelland. Reportedly this lead length delivered 90% of the maximum diving depth with lipped crankbaits.

McClelland's data is backed up with reams of graph paper that show conclusively how deep various lures will run when trolled on 120 feet of line. Although McClelland's data was well received, the 98 cent question became, how deep will these lures run on shorter or longer leads?

That question remained unanswered until a second book, Precision Trolling, researched and written by Michigan's Dr. Steve Holt, Tom Irwin and Mark Romanack took McClelland's data and crankbait trolling another step forward. The trio of anglers based their data on actual obser-

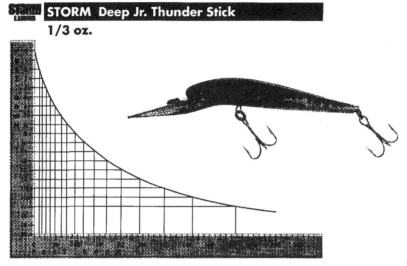

STORM Deep Jr. Thunder Stick

1/3 oz.

This dive curve taken from the book Precision Trolling shows how deep a Deep Jr. ThunderStick dives when fished on various leads and 10 pound test. Knowing how deep your lures are fishing is what precision trolling is all about.

vation of lures pulled past a scuba diver.

Each lure tested for the book Precision Trolling was pulled past a diver with 15, 30, 60, 90, 120, 150, 180, 200, 220 and 250 feet of line out. The depth ranges achieved using these leads were recorded and later plotted onto a graph the trio refer to as a dive curve. The dive curve clearly shows the downward diving angle for each crankbait, making it possible to quickly and accurately determine the exact lure diving depth for any lead length from 15 to 250-feet.

Next Holt, Irwin and Romanack superimposed a life-sized picture of the lure onto a dive curve printed with easy to read "feet down" and "feet back" measurements. The life-size picture of the crankbait makes positive lure identification easy. Even if you don't know what brand or model of lure you're using, the bait can be quickly identified by comparing the lure photos on various dive curves.

The dive curves are printed on heavy card stock. Connected together with a ring binder, the booklet is neatly bound and handy to use. Precision Trolling contains dive curves for 120 crankbaits including the most popular brands and models.

Both a paper and laminated pro version are available from Book Central, 20061 21 Mile Rd., Tustin, MI 49688. The paper version is $19.95 and the pro version runs $24.95 plus $4.50 shipping.

All the testing and dive curve data in Precision Trolling is based on 10 pound test monofilament. Those anglers who troll using lighter or heavier monofilament line can still determine lure diving depth accurately by adding or subtracting diving depth depending on line diameter.

"Those who troll with eight pound test line should add 10% to the depths listed in the dive curves," suggests Dr. Holt. "Those who fish 12 pound test should subtract 5%. Subtract 15% for lures trolled on 14 pound test and 25% for 17 pound test."

For example, a lure that's running 20 feet on 10 pound test will run at 22 feet (20 ft plus 2 ft) on eight pound test, but only 15 feet (20 ft minus 5 ft) on 17 pound test line.

Holt, Irwin and Romanack used Daiwa 27LC (line counter) reels to

Crankbaits come in all shapes, sizes and colors. A modest selection of baits including some minnow, shad and fat body profiles will insure success with a wide variety of species.

measure their lead lengths. "Each reel must be filled to capacity to get the most accurate readings," says Romanack. "A popular line counter reel, the 27LC reel holds up to 360 yards of 14 pound test monofilament. The 27LC holds enough line for most trolling applications. The exception to this rule occurs when fishing Dipsy Divers that require the larger 47LC model. The 47LC holds 280 yards of 20 pound test."

THE FACTORS OF LURE DEPTH

Regardless of which line you select, monitoring trolling lead is a critical element of precision crankbait trolling. However, lead length is only one of several factors that determine how deep a crankbait will dive. Line diameter, the amount of line out and the shape, lip size and buoyancy of the lure all combine to determine maximum diving depths.

The line diameter or pound test best for general trolling conditions is an often debated topic. Ideally a line suitable for trolling must be small enough in diameter to allow lures to dive deeply, while being strong enough to handle fish safely.

According to Holt, Irwin and Romanack, 10 pound test is the ideal line when trolling for small to medium sized fish such as walleye, bass, brown trout and northern pike. "Lines smaller in diameter than 10 pound test have too much stretch making it tough to get solid hooksets," comments Irwin. "Small diameter lines also abrade more easily and may fail at the worst possible moment."

"Lines larger than 10 pound test significantly reduce lure diving depth," claims Holt. "A 1/4 ounce Storm Hot 'N Tot maxes out it's dive curve at 15 feet on 10 pound test line. The same lure and lead combination fished on 17 pound test line will only dive to about 11 feet."

When fishing for large fish like salmon, lake trout, steelhead or stripers, heavier pound test line is essential. "While heavier line reduces the diving depth of crankbaits, the loss in diving depth can be off set to a degree by letting out longer trolling leads," explains Romanack. "A compromise in line diameter is the logical solution to this dilemma. Try 14 to 17 pound test when fishing for salmon or other powerful fish.

The amount of line let out is a strong influence on how deep a crankbait will dive. Holt, Irwin and Romanack experimented with lead lengths much longer than tested by McClelland. "In some cases we saw lures

41

Mark Romanack, a co-author of Precision Trolling says that within normal trolling speeds, lure depth is not influenced significantly. Lead length and line diameter are the primary forces that effect crankbait diving depth.

Crankbaits are most often used to catch warm water species such as walleye or bass, but they are equally effective on trout and salmon. Dr. Steve Holt, co-author of the book Precision Trolling caught this lake trout using the tips outlined in the chapter.

continuing to dive even after letting out 260 feet of line," claims Irwin. "The Luhr Jensen Powerdive Minnow is an excellent example. A lure with an extra large diving lip, the Powerdive achieved a depth of 25 feet with a 120 foot lead and 35 feet when trolled on a 260 foot lead."

"The Powerdive minnow picks up an additional 10 feet of diving depth when run on very long leads," adds Holt. "A significant depth improvement, this lure and other super deep divers are capable of reaching greater depths than we ever dreamed possible."

43

Ironically, not all big lipped lures turn out to be the deep divers they appear to be. The body size and buoyancy appears to have a major impact on how deep a lure will dive.

"The Rebel D-30 Spoonbill is a good example of a lure I expected to be a super deep diver," comments Irwin. "After testing the Spoonbill D-30 and learning that it only dives to 18 feet, I was sure the lure tested had to be out of tune. After testing several other D-30 Spoonbills, I finally came to the conclusion that this bait which appears to be a deep diver is actually a medium depth diving lure."

Large crankbaits with wide buoyant bodies tend to run slightly shallower than you might expect. Other big lipped lures that don't dive as deep as you might think include the Rapala No. 9 Shad Rap and Poe's Deadeye. Although each of these lures are excellent fish producers, they don't dive as deep as other lures with similar lip sizes.

TROLLING SPEED

It's a common misconception that trolling speed influences a crankbait's diving depth. It does not! Within the ranges of normal use, crankbaits will dive to the same depths regardless of lure speed. The exception of course are lures that are out of tune and not running properly.

Holt, Irwin and Romanack discovered that lures trolled at .75 to 3 MPH all achieved the same maximum depth, but lures trolled slowly took a little longer for the baits to reach maximum depth.

Trolling speed does however have a profound effect on lure action. Certain baits have little or no action at slow speeds and must be pulled at a brisk clip to be effective. Other baits simply can't be trolled fast or their subtle action is lost and the bait worthless.

The best way to determine the ideal trolling speed for individual baits is to observe them running near the boat. Place the crankbait in the water and adjust the trolling speed until the lure responds with the best possible action. Make sure the bait is tuned properly and running straight through the water. If the lure wants to run left or right, the bait needs to be tuned by bending the line tie in the opposite direction.

Tuning crankbaits is a tricky business. It takes patience and practice to determine the ideal action for each lure. Regardless of advertising claims, most brands and models of crankbaits need a little fine tuning to get the most action from each lure.

Crankbaits run best when attached to the line using a small fast lock snap. Make sure the snap used doesn't include a swivel and be sure the snap is rounded in shape so the lure has a free range of movement.

A polamar knot is the best way to attach a snap to monofilament fishing line. The strongest knot available and easy to tie, consult any package of fishing line for instructions on how to tie the polamar knot.

Line bow while trolling is another factor worth exploring. "I noticed during many dives that most of the monofilament on a long lead floats on the surface," commented Holt. "With diving crankbaits, only the last few feet of line angles down sharply to the lure. When trolling, a large bow of line forms between the rod tip and the lure."

Bow in the fishing line is a counter productive factor that makes it more difficult to hook fish while trolling. Before a fish that strikes a crankbait trolled on long leads can become hooked, the bow in the monofilament line must be pulled taunt.

"There's no doubt that walleyes routinely strike at passing crankbaits, but before the line pulls tight enough to set the hook they sense something is wrong and drop the bait," claims Romanack. "No one knows for sure how much this phenomenon occurs, or how many fish willing to bite are not hooked each trolling season."

There are several ways anglers can increase the odds of hooking the fish that bite. Trolling with the shortest leads possible helps to reduce the elapsed time between when a fish bites and the line pulls tight.

Anglers can also try trolling a little faster than normal when the fish are biting well, but are not getting hooked up solidly. A faster trolling speed also reduces the amount of elapsed time between the strike and hookup and works to set the hook with more authority.

Thirdly, using lines with a minimum amount of stretch is an advantage when trolling crankbaits. Wet monofilament line stretches like a rubber band, making it tough to set a hook solidly in the mouth of a walleye or other bony mouth fish.

Certain types of monofilament are formulated for low stretch. A new line from Stren known as Sensor has the lowest stretch of any monofilament line. This outstanding line for trolling has about 50% less stretch making for better hooksets and a higher ratio of landed fish.

Trolling with slightly heavier lines may also help reduce line stretch problems. Trolling with 12 pound test line reduces lure diving depth by approximately 5%, while significantly reducing line stretch problems associated with eight pound test line.

"There's no perfect system that guarantees fish that bite a crankbait are going to get hooked and landed," admits Holt. "I put the odds in my favor by using the sharpest possible hooks. Thin round bend style treble hooks stick, penetrate and hold better than hooks made from larger wire. These hooks are also soft enough that they can be bent out and the lure retrieved if it snags bottom."

The dive curve data prepared by Holt, Irwin and Romanack along with their fishing tips amount to a deadly system for trolling walleyes, pike, trout or any species that will strike a crankbait. "Crankbaits can be aimed at game fish that mark on a graph like a hunter aims his bullet," says Holt. "The secret to catching more fish is understanding how lead lengths influence lure depth and carefully putting your crankbaits where these trophies live."

With Precision Trolling as a guide, crankbait trolling isn't such a mystery to the average angler. In fact, there are three easy steps to successful crankbait trolling.

The first step is to locate fish with the help of your electronics. The second step requires the angler to select and try a variety of lures that will dive to the depths which correspond to fish marking on the graph. Patterning fish on crankbaits is as simple as selecting the proper lead length and seeing which baits the fish prefer.

The final step is an important one that many anglers lose sight of. Once a productive lead length and lure combination are determined, it's critical to reproduce this combination exactly with other lines. Adding more lines with identical lures and lead lengths completes the pattern. When you've reached this point, it's all down hill. The hard part is over and it's time to reap the benefits of precision trolling.

From crankbaits we move on to the subject of fishing open water spinners. This little known trolling technique is deadly on walleye, bass, trout and many other species.

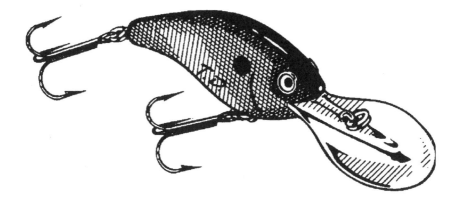

Captain Al Lesh is a trolling icon in the Great Lakes region. You'll most often find him walleye fishing on Lake Erie and Saginaw Bay.

Chapter 5

Trolling Open Water Spinners
By
Al Lesh

Open water fishing has for years been the exclusive domain of the crankbait and spoon troller. These lures used in combination with planer boards are a classic solution to the age old problem of patterning suspended fish. Trolling with cranks or spoons is undoubtedly one of the most effective ways to catch walleye, trout, salmon, striper, bass and even panfish like crappies when the fish are hot and biting readily. Unfortunately, for as good as these lures are during stable weather, they are often a disappointment when the weather turns sour.

Ironically, cold fronts don't prevent game fish from suspending, it simply makes them more selective in the their feeding habits. When a cold front hits you can forget about limit catches if your fishing cranks and spoons pulled 2-3 miles per hour, but you don't have to forget about limits.

A new style of trolling is making a splash in the sport fishing world. This new technique incorporates live bait into a deadly trolling presentation that works on walleye, bass, trout and other species even during cold front conditions.

Sound too good to be true? Trolling with spinner harnesses offers fish a slower presentation, the flash, vibration and color of a spinner blade plus a fat nightcrawler to sweeten the package! This combination adds up to rod bending action when crankbaits and spoons aren't producing.

The spinners used for open water trolling are a little more sophisticated than the garden variety nightcrawler harness available at sport shops. For one thing the harnesses used for trolling are longer, usually 48-60

49

inches long. Instead of three single hooks snelled in place on a monofilament leader, a single No. 2 beak style hook is snelled in the front and a No. 4 or 6 treble hook snelled at the back of the rig approximately five or six inches from the front hook.

The single hook is placed through the crawler's nose and the treble hook is positioned midway in the crawler. This hooking combination allows the crawler to pull straight in the water and offers a higher percentage of hooked and landed fish.

In front of the hooks a dozen colorful beads are threaded onto the leader, followed by a plastic quick change clevice that allows blade size, shape and color to be changed without cutting the harness.

The blades used for open water trolling are often larger than those used by the typical angler. Size No. 4, 5, 6, 7 and even 8 Colorado and Indiana style blades are used to lure in fish from great distances. Flashy genuine silver and gold plate blades are among the most popular colors, but chartreuse, green, orange and combinations of these colors also work.

The end of these open water harnesses are finished off with a ball bearing swivel that helps to prevent line twist. The ball bearing swivel is a small but important part of spinner trolling. Inexpensive swivels simply can't prevent line twist when trolling at speeds up to 1.5 mph.

Even the line used to tie these harnesses is unique. Stren produces a special leader material for salt water anglers known as High Impact Hard Mono. Salt water anglers use this leader material because it's bite proof. A growing number of open water trollers have discovered that this leader material is ideal for tying spinner harnesses because it is more durable than regular monofilament.

Hard Mono leader is clear and flexible enough to snell nicely, yet fish can't bite through or nick the line with their sharp teeth. A single spinner harness tied using this leader material will out last half a dozen harnesses tied on ordinary monofilament braided line harnesses. The new super braids are also useful for tying spinner harnesses.

These custom tied spinners must be weighted or otherwise rigged to make them run below the surface. One of the most popular methods of trolling spinners incorporates in-line sinkers known as Snap Weights.

A Snap Weight is an Off Shore Tackle OR-16 pinch pad line clip

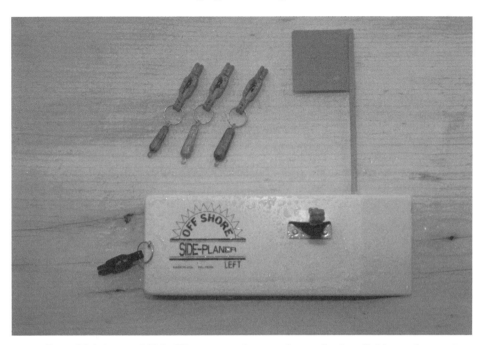

Snap Weights and Side-Planers are frequently used when fishing spinners in open water. Each product compliments the other making for a marriage that's deadly on suspended fish.

with a lead sinker attached. This line clip features a strong spring tension and rubber pads that hold the weight securely on the line until the angler reels up the weight and removes it.

Because the weight isn't permanently attached to the line, the weight can be attached anywhere between the lure and the rod tip. Positioning the weight 20, 30, 40 or even 50 feet ahead of the lure separates the lure from the weight and allows the bait to swim naturally.

When a fish is hooked the angler reels in the fish and Snap Weight until the weight can be removed by pinching open the line release. Once the weight is removed, the angler continues to fight the fish as normal.

A popular form of Snap Weight rigging is known as the 50/50 method. The spinner harness is let out behind the boat 50 feet, then a Snap Weight is attached to the line and another 50 feet of leader let out. This 100 foot trolling lead with a snap on weight positioned midway on the line can be fished as a flat line or attached to an in-line or catamaran style planer

51

board to increase lure coverage.

The fishing depth is regulated by using different size in-line weights and by manipulating speed. The best speeds for spinner trolling range from .5 to 1.5 miles per hour. If faster speeds are employed line twist can become a problem.

Most anglers find that a small gasoline kicker motor is ideal for maintaining these slower trolling speeds. Larger boats that don't have kicker motors can drag a sea bag or use trolling plates to reduce speed.

Snap Weight clips may be purchased two in a package or as a kit that contains four clips and an assortment of weights.

When setting up a Snap Weight trolling program, use several different weights so the trailing spinners are fishing at different depths. Once fish are located and a particular weight becomes productive, other lines can be switched over to the productive size weight.

Anglers who fish Snap Weights favor the Off Shore Tackle Side-Planer because this in-line board can handle up to three ounces of trolling weight. Other small skis simply aren't designed to pull Snap Weights or other heavy trolling hardware.

Snap-on weights are an efficient way of presenting spinners to suspended walleye, bass, trout and other species. Another spinner trolling technique employs a small diving planer known as a Jet Planer. Produced by Luhr Jensen the Jet Planer floats like a crankbait at rest and dives when trolled. Because this diver floats at rest and dives when trolled it is less speed sensitive than snap weights or weighted divers.

The diver is tied to the main line using a snap that fits in one of three line attachment holes and a spinner is attached to a swivel at the back of the diver. Diving depth is influenced by lead length and which hole the snap is placed in.

"When trolled on 10 pound test the Model 20 Jet Diver reaches a maximum depth of 18 feet when set on the bottom hole and trolled using a 150 foot lead," says Steve Holt a trolling expert and one of the authors of Precision Trolling. "The middle hole yields a maximum depth of 22 feet and on the top hole this diving plane will fish 30 feet below the surface."

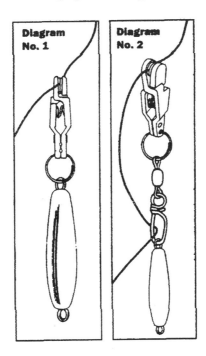

Smaller Snap Weights can be placed on the line as in diagram No. 1. For larger weights or when fishing near bottom the option shown in No. 2 is best.

Jet Divers can be fished at specific depths by simply altering the amount of trolling lead used. For depths ranging from 10-15 feet leads of 15-40 feet are used. For deeper results longer trolling leads are used.

This trolling style works best when several different trolling leads are used to search for fish at different depths. When a productive lead length is discovered, switch over other lines to duplicate the results.

The smaller size Jet Divers can be fished in combination with in-line planer boards. Larger Jet Divers have a considerable amount of drag in the water and are best suited to flatline trolling.

Lead core line is a third option for delivering spinners to suspended fish in open water. Lead core line features a core of soft lead wire covered with a coating of durable dacron. Lead core comes in different break strengths like monofilament. The size 18 and 27 pound test lead core are the most popular sizes.

A unique rigging method known as segmented lead core is used when

53

trolling spinners. Setting up a lead core outfit begins by spooling 200 yards of 10 to 17 pound test monofilament backing onto a large levelwind style reel. Next, the lead core is nail knotted to the monofilament backing and three colors or 90 feet of lead core is spooled onto the reel. The rig is completed by adding a 50 foot leader of 10 to 17 pound monofilament.

When fishing lead core and spinners, the rig is baited with a fat nightcrawler and fed out behind the boat until all the leader and lead core are out. The depth the lead core runs is controlled by trolling speed and how much backing is let out.

This segmented method of fishing lead core allows for maximum depth and allows in-line planer boards to be used for increased trolling coverage. Extra reels spooled with one or two colors of lead core offer even more trolling flexibility. More information about lead core trolling is offered in chapter 10.

All these trolling options are best suited to downrigger style rods and large levelwind reels. Line counter reels such as the Daiwa SG27LC are very popular among trollers who recognize the value of monitoring lead length. If you don't own line counter reels you can monitor lead length by using metered fishing lines or by counting how many times the line passes back and forth across the face of the spool when setting lines.

A guide for determining the running depth of Snap Weights, Jet Divers and lead core line is available in the book Precision Trolling. The data is based on actual under water observation of these trolling systems.

Fishing for open water walleye, bass or trout with spinner rigs is one of the hottest techniques going. An alternative to crankbait or spoons, spinners bring a new dimension to open water trolling.

Spinners and spoons have a lot in common. In the next chapter some of the nation's leading authorities on spoon trolling will share their secrets for catching walleye, salmon, trout and other species.

*Al Lesh is a charter captain and tournament pro with over 30 years of trolling experience.

Spinner Tying Tips

A lot of anglers enjoy tying their own spinners. Open water spinners can be tied with two single hooks, a single hook and a treble hook or two treble hooks. Spinners rigged with a treble hook(s) hold better on large or powerful fish.

Spinners should be tied using quality monofilament or a leader material such as Stren High Impact Hard Mono Leader. Braided lines can also be used to tie harnesses. Choose eight to 12 pound test for walleye and bass and 14 to 20 pound test for trout, pike and other large fish.

Snelling a crawler harness is easy. Cut a piece of monofilament or leader material 60 inches long and thread one end approximately an inch through the hook eye to be snelled. Pinch this short tag of line firmly against the hook shank with a thumb and forefinger and wrap the main line eight or 10 times around the hook shank. Hold these wraps firmly and then take the end of the main line and pass it back through the hook eye from the opposite direction as before. Hold the hook and wraps firmly until the leader can be pulled up tight.

Thread the second hook onto the leader and position it approximately six inches from the first hook. Pinch the line against the hook shank and snell this hook in the same manner as the first. This method of snelling is easy and allows the hooks to be positioned exactly the same distance apart every time.

Once the two hooks are snelled in place, add a dozen colorful beads, a clevice and the blade of choice. For open water fish size 4, 5, 6, 7 and 8 Colorado or Indiana style blades are best.

A size No. 2 beak hook and round bend treble hooks in size No. 6 and 4 are ideal for these harnesses.

Each spinner should be finished by adding a ball bearing swivel to the end. Quality swivels are cheap insurance against line twist.

55

The Eppinger Flutter Chuck spoon designed by Chuck Cartwright was one of the first lures desiged especially for Great Lakes trolling. He later went on to design the Wolverine Silver Streak, a spoon that has become a favorite of countless trollers.

Chapter 6

Spoon Trolling

By
Chuck Cartwright & Bill Sturm

DEVELOPING TROLLING SPOONS (Chuck Cartwright)

As fishing lures go, the Great Lakes style trolling spoon has come a long way in two decades. Serious spoon development started about the same time king and coho salmon were introduced into the Great Lakes, during the early 1970's. The demand for bigger catches of these popular fish fueled a desire to build spoons that offered a wider variety of trolling applications.

Unlike casting spoons, trolling spoons are lighter, thinner and have a more pronounced wobble. While casting spoons can be used in many trolling applications, the lighter trolling spoons dominate the big water.

The first salmon trolling spoons used in the Great Lakes were high speed lures that ran best at three MPH or faster. Designed to compliment popular lures of the day such as the J-Plug or Grizzly, spoons that would offer good action at slower speeds didn't appear for some time.

My first introduction to the spoon market came while I was working for Eppinger. The Flutter Chuck, still popular today, was designed to be a high speed spoon that would fish effectively at 2.5 to 3.5 MPH. Despite the popularity of the Flutter Chuck, it wasn't long after this lure came out that I realized there was a need for a more forgiving spoon. When I went back to the drawing board, my goal was to develop a spoon that could be trolled fast without spinning or at slow speeds and still have that deadly side-to-side wobbling action.

Building such a spoon proved to be no easy task. Several prototypes were built that simply didn't meet my goal. I worked on this project for about a year before I finally hit on the answer. Along the way the lure

57

Spoons come in an unending array of colors with equally colorful names. Expressive names like Monkey Puke, Doctor Death, Michael Jackson and Orange Crush are just a few of the popular color choices.

dies were ground and reground some more, extra cup was added to the spoon and a flat spot incorporated to give the lure a little extra kick. What materialized was the Silver Streak, a trolling spoon that has become one of the most popular and effective lures in the Great Lakes.

Today the Silver Streak is offered in four different sizes including the Micro, Mini, Regular and Mag versions. Ironically the Micro Streak was originally built as a ladies ear ring to be sold as a novelty item at consumer shows. Before long people were requesting that hooks be added and now the spoon is popular with walleye fishermen that use the spoon when trolling three way rigs in combination with a diving crankbait.

The Mini Streak was designed especially for walleye fishing. However, this little spoon also sees a lot of action with sliders or stackers among salmon and steelhead trollers.

The Regular Streak is my all time favorite and this lure has become a standard among Great Lakes trollers. Ideal in size for steelhead, lake trout, brown trout and salmon, this bait is our best selling model.

The Mag Streak was designed for lake trout trolling, but salmon fishermen swear by it. Personally, I rarely troll with the Mag Streak, but we have thousands of customers who troll little else.

SPOON COLOR

Once we had the basic design of the Silver Streak refined, the door was open to experiment with color and finishes. We use genuine silver plating on our spoons to generate the maximum amount of flash. Streak spoons are available that are painted, dressed with flash tape or a combination of these finishes. In total over 500 color variations are available and the list continues to grow.

Most of our existing color choices originally came from anglers who requested custom color patterns. Once a color establishes itself as a consistent producer it becomes a permanent part of our color chart.

Along the way we've built some unusual colors with some unusual names. Again we can't take credit for most of these names that are in many respects as colorful as the lures themselves. Names like Monkey Puke, Michael Jackson and Doctor Death are just a few of the color names that have developed over the years.

Naturally some colors have become more popular than others. A few of the top colors, based on product sales include Pink Alewife, Doctor Death, Monkey Puke, Michael Jackson, Holloween, Black Raspberry, Green Alewife, Watermelon, Yellowtail and Orange Crush.

Not always have I been able to predict which colors would be killers on fish and popular with anglers. Some years ago I introduced a color called Shiner that was a perfect match to the alewife. The lure featured a scale pattern along the bottom, but apparently no one liked it because the color sold poorly. Ultimately if a color doesn't get tried, it won't ever become a consistent fish producer.

The truth about spoon colors is they usually come and go in trends. As long as anglers come to us with new color patterns, we'll keep making lures that become the newest trends. We're always making new colors and creating baits that anglers swear by.

SPOONS AND DOWNRIGGERS

59

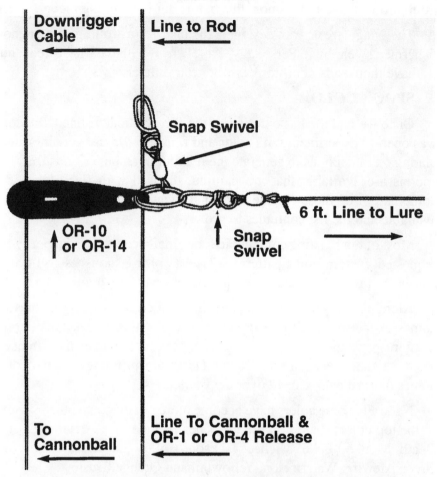

Downrigger Cable

Line to Rod

Snap Swivel

OR-10 or OR-14

Snap Swivel

6 ft. Line to Lure

To Cannonball

Line To Cannonball & OR-1 or OR-4 Release

This illustration shows a simple fixed slider. Fixing the slider insures that the lure runs at the proper depth and increases hook-up success.

Downriggers are one of the most effective ways to present trolling spoons for salmon, trout and walleye. The methods used to present spoons with downriggers is often debated. My attitude is simple, keep the leads short. I usually rig my spoons to run within 10 feet of the downrigger weight on the main line. If you're going to run stackers, set the main line back 15-20 feet and position the stacker five feet above the main line with a lead of five to 10 feet.

If sliders are used, keep the lead short, say five or six feet. Sliders can be fixed to the main line by simply threading an Off Shore Tackle OR14 planer board release onto the slider leader. The rig is simple. Start

King salmon are one of the most common targets of spoon trollers, but many other species can be taken with these universal lures including walleye, steelhead, brown trout, lake trout, pike and even bass.

with a six foot length of monofilament and tie a ball bearing swivel onto one end, then thread on the OR14 release and finish the rig by tying on another swivel. On one swivel clip on a spoon. The other swivel is clipped over the main line and the pinch pad release is attached to the main line to hold the slider wherever you want it.

Across the board the leads I run are short. Running these tight leads makes the boat more maneuverable. If you hit a school of fish, the boat can be turned quickly in order to get back onto the fish fast. With longer leads the boat must be turned more gradually to avoid tangling lines.

There's another advantage to fishing short leads. Using shorter leads means less line stretch, better hook-ups and fewer lost fish.

BOARDS AND SPOONS

In-line and catamaran style boards are also frequently used to present spoons near the surface for steelhead or kings, cohos and even lake trout when fishing the skum line or during the early season. When fishing spoons behind boards I recommend setting the baits back 40-50 feet. These lines can be fished clean when working the surface or weighted with a Snap Weight or a slip sinker weight in front of a barrel swivel to target fish a little below the surface.

SPOONS AND DIVERS

Divers are another valuable spoon fishing tool. When fishing Dipsy Divers keep leads short. I rarely fish a Dipsy more than 100 feet back and usually fish them 40-50 feet out.

If I use a Slide Diver, I bump my lead lengths up to 10-15 feet. This unique product allows the lead to be set at any length. When a fish strikes the diver triggers and slides down the line.

The Jons Diver dives a little sharper than other similar products on the market. I use this diver when I'm trying to keep my divers running tight to my downrigger lines, such as when I'm fishing in traffic or if the downriggers are producing especially well. Again I favor a six foot lead the same as when fishing a Dipsy.

ANOTHER SPOON FISHING PERSPECTIVE (Bill Sturm)

I've lived by and fished southern Lake Huron my whole life. Port Austin to Port Huron has been my stomping grounds for over 20 years, but I've also spent a good deal of time fishing Oscoda, Harrisville, Rogers City and Alpena. During that time I've seen a lot of changes take place in fishing techniques, but none as dramatic as the impact spoons have made in recent years.

Only a few years ago most salmon/trout fishermen started out the season using exclusively body baits such as the Bomber Long A and Storm ThunderStick. Today, I use a combination of spoons and body baits to start out the season and soon switch to running exclusively spoons.

On my boat — Gone Bad Charters — spoons have proven themselves at all speeds and at every time of year. There's simply not a day on the water that I don't find trolling spoons to be effective.

Part of my loyalty to spoons has come about because of superior designs that can be fished slower and still have excellent action. The Wolverine Silver Streak is a prime example of a spoon that can be fished at many speeds. Also, I find that the Stinger Spoon has similar characteristics. Both these spoons are available in four different sizes.

DEVELOPING A SPOON PATTERN

My strategy for fishing spoons is very simple. I begin by selecting a spoon size that matches as close as possible to the forage available. If smelt are abundant, such as during the early spring, I favor a standard sized spoon. During the summer when alewife are the primary forage, the larger magnum sized spoons work best for me. When using sliders or stackers, I normally select a slightly smaller sized spoon.

The next step is to decide upon some confidence colors to start with. Usually I select my spoon colors based on the water color. Early in the day, I lean heavily towards dark colors such as purple, brown, black and green. These colors also work well in stained or off color water.

During the brightest parts of the day, I've had my best success with softer colors such as pearl, white, chartreuse, lime green and silver.

The third element of my spoon strategy is speed. I'm a stickler for fishing speeds that seem to produce the best possible action from my lures. Normally I'll fish from 2.5 to 3.5 MPH, but given the opportunity I'll most often fish as close to 2.7 MPH as possible.

Controlling your speed is easy on calm days, but when the wind picks up it's much more difficult to maintain a specific speed. You can control your speed best by trolling downwind. Unfortunately, sometimes the underwater currents make it tough to fish with the wind. I monitor underwater currents by watching the cable sway of my downriggers. When cross currents pose a problem, I'll adjust my trolling direction to run with the underwater current or give up and try fishing another area.

SLIDERS OR STACKERS

I use a free slider frequently because they are a simple way of adding an additional lure in the water for each line fished. If I don't have a strong commitment to a particular depth zone, a slider makes sense because they are free to move up and down on the main line. The spoon used on the slider is usually one size smaller than the one used on my main line.

A fixed slider or a stacker is a better option when fishing a specific depth zone. The Off Shore Tackle OR2 medium tension stacker release is an absolute must when fishing two rods on a single downrigger. This effective release incorporates two downrigger style releases mounted onto a coated cable. The release on the short lead is attached to the downrigger cable at the depth desired and the longer lead is clipped to the fishing line.

I usually run my stackers five feet above the main line and set a trolling lead of only five or six feet. Keeping the stacker leads short helps to prevent tangles with the stacker and main line when fish are hooked.

I run stackers a lot with a spoon while trolling a dodger and squid combination on the main line. Using this combination allows me to keep some spoons in the program even when dodgers are the primary focus.

LINES AND OTHER TROLLING TRICKS

I fish lighter line than most charter captains. Most of my rods are rigged with 15 pound test. Occasionally I'll use up to 20 pound test, if I'm fishing hardware like dodgers.

On my diver rods I start out the season with 15 pound test to achieve the best possible depth with the shortest leads. During the summer I'll switch over to 20 pound test or in some cases spool up with wire line.

Spoon Trolling

Wire line is the ultimate material for getting maximum depth from a diver. The problem with wire is it can be tricky to fish with, especially for those anglers who aren't familiar with it. My advice with wire is to play with it on one rod until you become confident enough to spool up several more reels.

Divers are my in between lines, used mostly to fill holes in my trolling pattern between in-line boards and downriggers. On most days I'll run at least two divers equipped with spoons, but if the diver rods start producing fish, I don't hesitate to stack two divers per side and pull out a couple downrigger or planer lines.

One of the things that amazes me most about spoon trolling is how one lure can catch fish like crazy, while other spoons that are seemingly the exact size and color produce little or nothing. I can't explain why some spoons work better than others, but I can sort out the best ones and keep them ready for action.

When a spoon proves itself as a fish catcher, it gets stored in a separate tackle box with other baits that are also consistent producers. These confidence baits get used every day on the water. Meanwhile I use new baits and new colors or lures that haven't proved themselves as experimental lines. When one of these experimental lures starts snapping fish, it gets moved up to the box that contains my confidence lures.

I've also discovered that you can get a little more kick from most spoons by replacing the split ring with one a size larger. The larger split ring gives the hook a little more freedom of movement and can open up the action of certain spoons.

Spoons come in a lot of sizes, shapes, colors and brands. Effective on a wide variety of species and in many trolling situations, spoons have become the number one trolling lure on the Great Lakes and that honor isn't likely to topple any time soon.

In the next chapter we'll get more detailed on the topic of fishing diving planers. Divers are a useful and popular trolling tool that can be used to catch just about anything that swims.

Chuck Cartwright owns Wolverine Tackle Company producers of Silver Streak Spoons. Bill Sturm is a 20 year veteran of charter fishing.

The author's brother Mike Romanack caught this dandy walleye while trolling a spinner rig behind a Dipsy Diver in Lake Erie. Divers are one of the most efficient ways of reaching depths down to 50 or 60 feet.

Chapter 7
Divers Down
By
Mark Romanack

When divers are down, the odds of catching fish are up. An intrical part of the trolling scene for 25 years, diving planers or what are more simply called divers are invaluable tools for the angler who enjoys trolling. Available in dozens of models, sizes, shapes and colors, there's a diver for every trolling situation. Trout, salmon, musky, northern pike, walleye and even bass are vulnerable to the depth and lure control provided by a diving plane.

Divers are available in a wide variety of sizes and shapes, but most fit into two categories including those that operate using a trip mechanism and others that are fixed to the line without a trigger or tripping mechanism. Both versions are useful trolling aids when fishing spoons, stickbaits, trolling flies, spinners, dodgers, flashers, gang spinners and other trolling hardware.

TRIP ARM DIVERS

Trip mechanism divers are characterized by the popular Luhr Jensen Dipsy Diver and the newer Slide-Diver. Both these products are available in two different sizes and with removeable plastic rings that increase the surface area and diving range.

One of the oldest and most accepted divers on the market, the Dipsy features a tow arm that can be adjusted to release at different tension settings suitable for fish of various sizes. A simple set screw is used to adjust the trip arm tension.

The Slide-Diver also uses an adjustable trip arm mechanism. There's a major difference however between these two fine products. The Dipsy is designed to accept a short leader that runs from the back of the diver to

67

Divers come in many different shapes, sizes and colors. This collection represents only a few of those available to choose from.

the lure. This leader is usually equal to the rod length used.

The Slide-Diver is threaded onto the line and can be positioned anywhere on the fishing line. Instead of forcing anglers to fish with short leaders, the Slide-Diver makes it practical to separate the diver from the lure. This unique feature has endless applications for open water trolling situations.

Both the Dipsy and Slide-Diver perform a similar function. Some anglers argue that when the diver is set near the lure it acts as an attractor. Others state that the diver may actually spook fish and that the best situation occurs when the diver is positioned well away from the lure. The jury is still out on this issue and a clear determination won't be rendered anytime soon.

Despite their obvious differences, both the Dipsy and Slide-Diver perform the same service for trollers. When the tow arm is snapped into the set position, the diver bites against the surface of the water and is forced to dive. When a fish strikes, the tow arm release mechanism snaps open and the angler is free to fight the fish without fighting the drag of the diver.

The Slide-Diver slides down the line after it releases. To prevent the diver from potentially knocking the fish off, a Speedo bead or barrel swivel is added to the line a few feet in front of the lure.

The Dipsy and Slide-Diver are also directional divers. A weight mounted on the bottom of the diving surface can be rotated left or right of center causing the device to plane out to the side of the boat as well as down below the surface. This unique feature increases the trolling coverage possible with divers and helps to position lures in water that hasn't been disturbed by the boat.

It's important to note that the directional feature on divers allows these products to reach out from the boat a modest distance. Directional divers are not a substitute for planer boards, but they do increase lure coverage and enjoy a solid niche in the trolling world.

The fishing depth of these and other divers is controlled by how much line is let out, line diameter, trolling speed and the directional setting selected. The amount of line out or the trolling lead used is the most significant factor in determining overall depth. The more line let out the deeper a diver will fish below the surface. However, there is a point of deminishing return. If too much line is let out, line stretch makes it more difficult to achieve good hook-sets and to trip the diver.

Most divers function best when fished on leads less than 150 feet. Many avid diver fishermen rarely set their lines further back than 60 feet.

Line diameter and speed collectively influence diver depth. The thinner line that's used the less drag that occurs in the water while trolling. Also since divers are negatively buoyant (they sink) speed plays a minor part in depth control. At slow speeds sinking divers will run slightly deeper than the same diver fished on the same lead length at faster speeds.

For practical purposes large divers such as the Dipsy or Slide-Diver

69

Young Tommy Kavajecz is all smiles over this nice king salmon taken on his Grand Father's boat the Fisherman. Tommy caught his prize using a Slide-Diver near the port of Two Rivers, Wisconsin.

should be fished on monofilament line from 15 to 30 pound test. To achieve maximum depth, some anglers use the new super braids or even stranded wire. Braided line and wire is much thinner than similar break strength monofilament. These products can be used with the Dipsy, but the Slide-Diver is designed to be used with monofilament lines.

The directional setting is the final factor in diver depth control. When the directional setting is set at the number zero, the diver runs straight down and achieves the maximum depth per lead length. If the directional setting is adjusted to the number one setting, the diver planes out to the side slightly sacraficing only a modest amount of overall depth. At the number three setting, the diver planes out to the side considerably and sacrafices a significant amount of its depth diving ability.

When using the directional setting on divers, some additional depth can be achieved by simply increasing the lead length. However, lead length alone can't make up entirely for depth lost when using the directional settings. When maximum depth must be achieved at the diretional settings, braided lines make the most sense. When using braided lines, it's critical to also use an in-line snubber to reduce the chances of a powerful fish snapping the line or tearing the hooks out of its mouth.

The book Precision Trolling shows the diving depth of the Dipsy Diver (both the No. 0 and No. 1 models) on all three directional settings and at lead lengths out to 150 feet. Priceless data, the dive curves provided by this publication make it possible to fish these divers with amazing accuracy and confidence.

FIXED DIVERS

A number of divers function without the benefit of trip arm mechanisms. Most of these products are smaller in size than trip arm divers. Because of their modest size most of these products do not create a significant amount of drag in the water and can be fished using lighter lines. Some of the popular models include the Mini Dipsy size 3/0, Big Jon Diver Disk, Luhr Jensen Jet Diver and Fish Seeker.

Because these divers are small in size, they are best suited to trolling lightweight lures such as flutter spoons, trolling flies, spinners and stickbaits. Diving style crankbaits should not be used with diving planers. Fixed divers can be fished as flat lines or used in combination with

71

in-line boards and dual ski boards to improve trolling coverage.

All of these products are negatively buoyant except the Jet Diver that floats at rest and dives much like a crankbait when trolled. The amount of line let out and the diameter of the fishing line used are the two factors that in part determine diving depth with a Jet Diver. The depth range is also adjusted by placing a snap into one of three holes or tow points positioned on the front of the diver. The bottom hole causes the device to run shallow, the middle hole a little deeper and the top hole deeper yet. These unique features makes the Jet Diver the most forgiving, flexible and predictable diver on the market.

Jet divers come in several sizes and each size offers an adjustable depth range. The smaller sizes are suitable for use with in-line boards and shallow water fishing situations. According to Precision Trolling, the Model 20 Jet Diver rigged on the top hole achieves a maximum depth of 30 feet when fished 150 feet behind the boat on 10 pound test line. The larger size Jet Divers achieve much deeper depths and must be run as flat lines or in combination with larger dual planer board skis.

Like the Dipsy, Jet Divers accept a short leader that runs to the lure. The length of this leader should not exceed rod length.

The Mini Dipsy and the Big Jon Mini Disk are smaller versions of popular trip arm divers. Both of these products feature a fixed tow point, and a directional setting. Suitable for use with light line, in-line boards and dual planer boards, these products fill a shallow water niche for species such as walleye, steelhead and brown trout that are often caught within 30 feet of the surface.

The Fish Seeker incorporates several different line attachment points that influence the depth levels achieved. These attachment points, line diameter and lead length are the three primary factors that influence depth. The Fish Seeker like all other divers performs best when line counter reels are used to monitor the lead lengths used.

Once a productive lead length is determined, it's a simple step to set other lines using the same lures, colors and lead lengths. Simple so long as you are equipped with line counter style reels.

The Daiwa SG27LC and SG47LC reels are the flag ship of line counters. These reels feature a gear driven counter that's durable and accurate. Daiwa also produces an electronic line counter reel that costs about twice as much for anglers who insist upon the best. Several new comers in the line counter market are also available.

Penn recently introduced their model 855, 875 and 895 line counter reels. These reels feature an electronic liquid crystal display screen that records in feet, a bait clicker, star drag and graphite frame. The Penn reels retail for $150.00 to $190.00 each.

Shimano, Marado and South Bend are also producing line counter reels for trollers who demand them and no doubt more companies will soon jump on the band wagon.

Diving planers are a simple and effective way to troll with many lures or live baits. Effective on just about anything that swims, divers see the most action for Great Lakes salmon, steelhead, trout and wall-eye, but they can be used to catch a wide variety of other species.

In the next chapter the focus switches to downriggers and methods for fishing these trolling aids for walleye, salmon, striper and more.

Bruce DeShano is a salmon pro who turned his attention towards walleye. One of the leading anglers on the PWT circuit, Bruce's knowledge of trolling has made him a top stick on the walleye circuit.

Chapter 8
Mastering Downriggers
By
Larry Hartwick & Bruce DeShano

Downrigger fishermen are the masters of deep water, shallow water and everything in between. Imagine what fishing in the Great Lakes and other large bodies of water would be like without downriggers. Now picture yourself fishing deep water species such as lake trout minus the depth control we take for granted when fishing downriggers.

In many fishing situations and for many species, downriggers are the only logical solution to catching fish. Most often thought of as deep water fishing tools, downriggers are also ideal for positioning lures close to the surface. This is especially true when fishing the Great Lakes for early and late season steelhead, brown trout and salmon or when working over large schools of stripers in southern impoundments. At certain times of year, these species are often located within 30 feet of the surface and downriggers are one of the most effective ways to catch them.

Downriggers are also capable of presenting a wide variety of lures with absolute accuracy. Precise lure placement is critical when fishing thermoclines or temperature breaks for summer salmon or trout. Downriggers are also the ticket when it' necessary to skim lures along the bottom for lake trout or structure loving walleye.

These are just a few species and angling situations downrigger fishermen commonly encounter, but the list doesn't stop here. Northern pike, musky and even bass are just as vulnerable to the style of depth control fishing only downriggers can provide.

What's even better is that anyone can master the use of downriggers and expand their fishing horizons. Getting started requires a modest amount of equipment, a little know how and the willingness to put both

75

to work catching fish.

MANUAL OR ELECTRICS?

Do I need expensive electric riggers? One of the most frequently asked questions among anglers shopping for downriggers, the answer may surprise you. When selecting downriggers most anglers are best served with quality manual operated units.

A set of two manual downriggers is a great place to start the process of learning how to fish downriggers. Most of the time downriggers are used to catch fish within 60 feet of the surface. Manual units such as Riviera's Model 300, 500 and 700 meet the needs of trollers after a wide variety of species.

Manuals make the most sense on small boats or for anglers who only expect to use downriggers occasionally. Dependable, functional and affordable, a good manual downrigger should include a slip clutch design, digital counter, rod holder(s), swivel arm, mounting hardware and approximately 200 feet of cable. Riviera brand manual riggers start at around $150.00 and range up to $250.00 each.

The oldest commercially built downriggers in America, the Riviera brand has survived the test of time. A simple and sturdy design is what separates the Riviera from other brands. The large polycarbonate reel is the trademark of Riviera Downriggers. Each turn of the handle picks up two feet of cable, making the process of setting lines twice as fast as competitive models.

Riviera downriggers are also built to last for decades. In fact, many of the riggers sold over 25 years ago are still in service. The Riviera plant in Port Austin can also upgrade older model downriggers with the new super tough polycarbonate reels and aluminum arms. You can even convert a manual unit into an electric for little more than the cost of the motor.

Electric downriggers enjoy a strong niche market. Any time fishing success depends on running the maximum number of lines, electric riggers are the most efficient tool for the job.

Boats rigged for Great Lakes trolling are good examples of situations where electric riggers shine best. Great Lakes boats typically incorporate

76

five electric downriggers to maximize lure coverage. A rigger is positioned to fish off both the port and starboard sides, two riggers are mounted near the corners and are positioned to fish straight out the back, plus a fifth rigger gets mounted in the middle of the transom. With so many downriggers in service, electrics are the only logical choice.

A boat equipped with five electric downriggers can easily handle up to 10 different lines, plus another 10 sliders for a grand total of 20 lures in the water at once! This bread-and-butter angling strategy is one of the reasons downrigger fishing is so effective. What other fishing technique is capable of running so many lines and lures with absolutely precise depth placement?

DOWNRIGGER ACCESSORIES

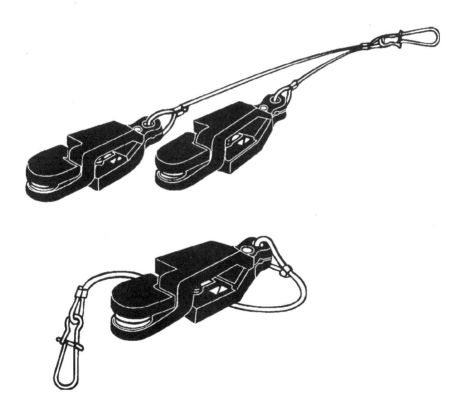

Pinch pad style stacker releases (top) and cannon ball releases (bottom) are invaluable downrigger trolling accessories. Off Shore Tackle manufactures a wealth of releases for different applications and species.

Downriggers are only as effective as their weakest link. That's why a quality downrigger deserves to be equipped with the best possible accessories.

Each rigger must be equipped with a downrigger weight for each rigger, plus at least one spare. A wide variety of shapes and size weights are available. A round ball with a small fin on the back is hard to beat for most downrigger fishing situations.

For salmon and deep water trout fishing a 10 pound ball is ideal for trolling speeds ranging from 2 - 4 MPH. Walleye fishermen who fish less than 50 or 60 feet below the surface can get by nicely with eight or 10 pound balls.

There's also a place for smaller four or six pound weights. Lighter weights are handy when slow trolling for early and late season walleye or when a school of young kings or pink salmon are located. The lighter weights makes it easier to detect strikes from these smaller fish.

Every boat should also carry a spare downrigger weight and cable termination kit. Sooner or later the weight is going to get caught on bottom and lost. If you keep a few simple tools, a spare termination kit and an extra weight on board, getting back into the action only takes a few minutes.

Quality downrigger releases are another critical accessory. An area where anglers commonly try to cut corners and save a few bucks, using rubber bands or aligator clip style releases is one of the leading reasons fish are often hooked and then lost with downriggers. Anyone who uses these poorly designed downrigger accessories are fooling themselves and losing fish needlessly.

Off Shore Tackle is the industry leader in pinch pad style downrigger releases. Each release produced by Off Shore Tackle represents hundreds of hours of one-the-water testing and product development. Designed to hold the line firmly yet gently, when a fish strikes, the pinch pad design provides enough tension to insure the fish is hooked solidly before releasing. It may sound obvious, but a line release must also be gentle on the fishing line. A lot of line releases out there can weaken the line seriously and lead to unnecessary break-offs

The model OR-1 medium tension release has become the standard

Trophy lake trout like this one taken by Wisconsin angler Don Parsons often fall prey to anglers who fish with downriggers.

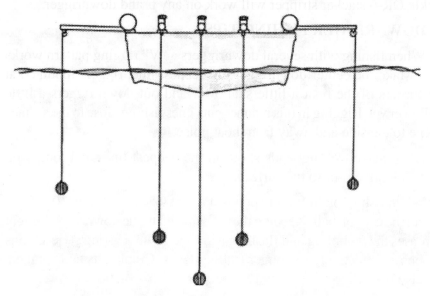

When fishing downriggers keep your trolling pattern simple. A "V" pattern that positions deeper lines near the center of the boat and more shallow lines near the edges of the boat works best.

pinch pad style release among salmon, trout and steelhead anglers. Walleye and brown trout anglers will find the OR-4 light tension release perfect for these sometimes small and often light hitting fish. The OR-8 heavy tension release is designed for trolling cowbells, dodgers or for powerful fish such as trophy salmon, musky and salt water species.

Line stackers are another invaluable accessory for downrigger fishing. Stackers allow two lines to be fished using a single downrigger. The second line is normally run five to 20 feet above the main line to increase lure coverage.

Off Shore Tackle offers two stackers including the OR-7 light tension for walleye fishing and the OR-2 medium tension for salmon, trout, steelhead and other larger species. When using these stackers be sure to secure the short arm release to the downrigger cable and the long arm release to the fishing line.

A stacker stripper/weight retriever automatically clears stackers from the downrigger cable when the ball is raised. This product also makes it easier to reach downrigger weights when resetting lines. The Off Shore

Tackle OR-6 stacker stripper will work on any brand downrigger.

DOWNRIGGER FISHING TIPS

When fishing with several downriggers a "V" rigging pattern works well. Make the center downrigger the deepest line, riggers mounted at the corners of the boat a little shallower and out-down riggers a little shallower yet. Rigging in this manner puts lines fishing close to the surface a little to the side and away from boat noise.

Also, make trolling leads short on the deepest lines and longer on lures running closer to the surface.

When fishing light flutter spoons it's best to set the spoon 10-20 feet behind the cannon ball. Keeping these baits tight to the downrigger weight increases the wobbling and flashing action. Heavier casting style spoons can be run effectively on longer trolling leads. Crankbaits and spinners can also be set further back without disturbing lure action.

Walleye anglers often run crankbaits 50-100 feet behind the downrigger weight. Using these longer leads allows the bait to dive below the downrigger weight and fish undisturbed water.

Downrigger fishing is an excellent way to cover all water depths and target a wide variety of species. A little equipment and know how is your license to get down and dirty with your favorite species.

In chapter nine the focus switches from trolling in large open bodies of water to trolling in current. Few anglers have discovered how effective trolling in rivers can be. Bass, walleye, sauger, pike and musky are all likely targets for the river troller.

Larry Hartwick is the master mind at Riviera Downriggers and a salmon tournament pro.

Big walleye like this one taken by Jim Morton are common catches for anglers that troll crankbaits in rivers.

Chapter 9
Trolling Crankbaits in Rivers
By
Dr. Steve Holt

Take a look at the big picture in sport fishing. Hardly a body of water or region has escaped the fact that trolling is the best way to both locate and catch fish. One area however stands as a challenge to the obvious virtues of trolling. Rivers are the last great fishing frontier and one of the few places that anglers rarely troll to catch fish.

Drifting with the current or fishing from an anchored position are the most popular ways of fishing rivers. Tradition more than common sense dictates why anglers don't consider trolling as an alternative method for fishing rivers.

WHY TROLL?

Considering the fact that drifting or anchoring is productive most of the time, why troll in rivers? Trolling, especially upstream trolling, has some subtle advantages over most other fishing presentations. First off, trolling against the current enables the angler to speed up or slow down the presentation as conditions dictate. In clear water when fish can see approaching baits from a considerable distance, trolling at a brisk pace covers water quickly while still producing strikes. When the water is dirty or turbid, slowing down gives fish a better opportunity to strike at passing lures.

Secondly, the lures used for trolling such as crankbaits are larger and make more noise in the water than jigs and other traditional river fishing lures. Not surprisingly, crankbaits are easier for bass, walleye, steelhead, trout and other species to locate and catch in the murky river environment. The more the water becomes stained or off color, the more

83

crankbaits excel and jig fishing suffers.

Thirdly, upstream trolling assures that lures will be running in the strike zone 100% of the time. This is especially true with floating/diving style crankbaits. With most jigging presentations the lure passes in and out of the strike zone as the angler pumps the rod handle. Snags are common and anglers spend all their time rigging and retying on new lures.

When upstream trolling the crankbait wiggles its way along within inches of bottom. If the lure fouls with weeds, leaves, small twigs or other debris, the vibration of the crankbait immediately stops tipping off the angler that the line needs to be checked and the bait cleaned of debris.

Snagged cranks are less of a problem than one might expect. So long as floating/diving style cranks are used, baits hung on bottom can be usually freed by simply giving the lure some slack line. The buoyancy of the lure and the rushing current work together to free most snags.

TOOLS OF THE TRADE

A few pieces of equipment are essential to upstream trolling success. A dependable gasoline kicker motor or powerful electric motor will be needed to pull the boat upstream against the current.

Quality and lightweight graphite rods and reels are a big advantage because the angler often spends long hours holding the rod and reel. For some trolling applications long rods such as those used for steelhead fishing are a big advantage. The longer rods reach out away from the boat and improve trolling coverage substantially.

Thin diameter fishing lines make the chore of keeping in contact with the bottom much easier. Either monofilaments that have been formulated to be extra thin in diameter or the latest generation of super braided lines can be used effectively when river trolling.

Crankbaits are the workhorse lures for river trolling. The best models for river fishing are those that float at rest and dive when trolled. An assortment of shallow, medium and deep divers will be required to cover all situations. In clear water conditions natural color baits produce the best. In murky waters brightly colored baits and those that feature rattles become more productive.

RIGGING UP

Upstream trollers have two primary rigging options to choose from. When fishing river flats and other areas where a slow to moderate current exists, floating/diving style crankbaits can be tied directly to monofilament or braided lines and trolled behind the boat. This method works best in waters 10 feet deep or less.

A wide assortment of floating diving crankbaits can be used effectively for upstream walleye trolling. Anglers may be surprised to find that it takes a fairly deep diving lure to reach bottom in just six feet of water when trolling against the current. The force of the current on the line and lure reduces the normal diving depth of crankbaits substantially.

The most popular choices are those baits that normally dive from 10-20 feet when trolled in still water. A few of the baits to consider include the Storm Wiggle Wart and 1/4 ounce Hot 'N Tot, Fred Arbogast Mud Bug, Rebel Wee R series, Cotton Cordell Wally Diver & CC Shad, Bomber 6A, Luhr Jensen 1/4 ounce Hot Lips and Rapala No. 7 Shad Rap. There are many other excellent choices.

In areas where the current is swift or the water deep, diving style crankbaits simply can't reach the bottom. A three way rig armed with a shallow diving crankbait is the answer in fast and deep river water.

A 12-inch dropper is used with a lead weight heavy enough to easily feel bottom. The monofilament used to tie the dropper should be at least one break strength lighter than the main line. If the sinker becomes snagged, the angler can break it off without losing the leader and the valuable crankbait.

The leader on the three way rig should be three to five feet long. Shallow diving minnow baits are the best cranks for use with this rig. Excellent suggestions include the Rapala No. 13 Floating Minnow, Storm Jr. ThunderStick, Bomber Long A and Smithwick Rattlin' Rogue. Fat bodied shallow divers may also be used in connection with a three way rig. The Luhr Jensen Speed Trap, Normark Shallow Shad Rap, Storm Thin Fin, Mann's 1 Minus and Bomber 2A are good choices.

HOW IT'S DONE

River flats often attract scattered schools of bass, walleye and other species. Upstream trolling with cranks is one of the fastest and most

A simple three way rig was used to present this shallow diving crankbait near bottom in deep and swift water.

efficient ways of covering this water. A small gasoline motor is a work-horse for this kind of fishing, but a powerful electric motor may also be used if the current isn't too strong.

Depending on the size of the area to be fished, it may require several passes to completely cover all the places fish may be hiding. Select a floating/diving style crankbait that will easily reach bottom when trolled 20-50 feet behind the boat. Let out line until you can feel the bait ticking bottom then shorten up the lead until the bait runs just over bottom. Too long a lead will cause the lure to simply scour into the bottom and quickly snag up.

Vary the trolling speed depending on conditions. In cold or murky waters a trolling speed that barely makes headway against the current is usually best. Once the water warms to near 50 degrees, a faster trolling speed may trigger reactionary strikes from actively feeding fish. A faster trolling speed also has the advantage of allowing the angler to cover water quickly.

In high water conditions, expect to find fish feeding very close to the bank. Areas to look for include spots where three to six feet of water can be located tight against the bank. Game fish herd minnows into these areas where they pin them against the shoreline, blocking their escape.

Slight depressions in the bottom will also hold fish. A depression in the bottom will show up readily on a quality liquid crystal graph. While the fish using these spots may be belly to bottom and tough to mark on the graph, fish these areas throughly and make a mental note of their location for future trips.

Sunken logs, rocks and other debris in the water are also good places to find fish waiting for their next meal. All these areas can be described as current breaks. Any place the flow of the current is disturbed by an object in the water or change in bottom contour, fish find sanctuary from the force of flowing water.

When a fish strikes, set the hook with a sharp rod sweep and imme-diately put the boat in neutral. Fight the fish as the boat slowly drifts downstream, watching that the boat doesn't drift into debris. Once the fish is landed, the boat is in position to make another pass through the same area.

River areas that feature a strong current or deep water are best fished with a three way rig and shallow diving crankbait. Three way rigs, often referred to as a Wolf River rigs are most effective when fishing deep river holes, long deep runs and riffles or other fast moving current areas.

The rig itself should be equipped with a lead weight that's heavy enough to make it easy to maintain contact with bottom. The angler doesn't drag the weight along bottom, but rather uses the weight to touch bottom every few feet while trolling. This touch-and-go fishing style insures that the trailing crankbait is positioned close to the bottom but above debris and other snags.

Depending on the water depth, trolling speed and depth of the water, the sinkers required for three way rigging may vary from 1/4 ounce to three ounces or more. When small weights are used a medium action spinning outfit makes a great rod for three way trolling. If heavier weights must be used to maintain contact with the bottom, stout medium or medium/heavy action baitcasting tackle is recommended.

Three way rigs may be trolled using a small gasoline motor or a powerful electric motor. In shallow water, a silent electric motor may be required to prevent spooking fish with motor noise. Small aluminum boats can get by nicely with a 12 volt electric motor that generates 35-40 pounds of thrust. Larger boats may require the extra thrust and battery life of a 24 volt system. The new 36 volt electric trolling motors like MotorGuide's Beast provide up to 70 pounds of thrust by tapping into extra power provided by the cranking battery in your boat.

When upstream trolling with an electric motor, bow mounted units are recommended over a transom mounted electric. It's easier to control the boat by dragging it upstream with the help of a bow mounted motor than by pushing it upstream with a transom mounted unit.

In many cases it will be necessary to use a small gasoline motor to power the boat upstream. Kicker motors are the most efficient way to troll upstream against strong current.

When using a kicker motor, the angler will need to keep one hand glued to the control handle at all times to keep the boat on course. When both hands are needed to tie on lures or other tasks, put the motor in neutral and drift downstream with the current until ready to fish again.

These anglers are teaming up to fight a fish hooked on the Detroit River. The Detroit River is one of the few places that upstream trolling is popular.

A new product designed for those who fish with kicker motors can help solve the boat control problems associated with trolling. An auto-pilot designed to mount on six to 15 horse power outboard motors, the Nautamatic TR-1 incorporates a simple hydraulic system and electronic compass to keep the boat on coarse in wind, waves and current.

The compass senses changes in the boat coarse and sends a message to the hydraulic system to move the motor accordingly. Fast and responsive, the system can also be controlled with a hand-held remote that allows changes in the course to be made by simply rotating the steering knob.

Upstream trolling with three way rigs or diving style crankbaits provides anglers with a new twist on river fishing. Jigs may be the most popular river fishing lures, but crankbaits and trolling also have their place in rivers.

The next chapter deals with some special trolling hardware known as lead core and wire line. The heavy metals of trolling, there's lots to know about these fish catching systems.

*Steve Holt is the co-author of Precision Trolling and a tournament walleye pro.

Chapter 10

Trolling Heavy Metal
By
Sam Anderson & Don Parsons

This outstanding walleye was taken with a crankbait fished on segmented lead core line.

Two of the oldest methods for getting lures deep are still popular and productive ways of catching walleye, salmon, trout and other species. Trolling with lead core and wire line enables anglers to fish shallow running lures such as stickbaits, spoons and spinners at depths that sometimes exceed 100 feet! These heavy metal trolling tactics aren't a substitute for downrigger fishing, but rather another presentation option. With a little ingenuity, it's amazing what anglers can accomplish with fishing lines that sink.

LEAD CORE LINE (Sam Anderson)

For those who haven't used it, lead core line is a flexible soft lead wire with a protective and durable covering of Dacron. Available in different sizes or break strengths similar to monofilament, the most common sizes of lead core are 15, 18 and 27. The lighter sizes are most often used for fishing walleye or trout found in inland lakes, while the heavier size is most popular for salmon, steelhead and striper.

Lead core is marked with a different color Dacron coating every 10 yards. Sometimes referred to as colors, marking the line in this fashion makes it easier to keep track of trolling leads and to duplicate effective lead and lure combinations.

While lead core is flexible enough to easily spool up on a heavy duty baitcasting or levelwind reel, it's not suitable for tying directly to fishing lures. Depending on the trolling application, a monofilament leader ranging from six to 50 feet is employed. Depending on the target species, the monofilament leader may range from 10 to 20 pound test.

FULL LEAD CORE

Lead core line can be rigged in a number of ways. One of the most common rigging methods is known as full lead core because the reel is completely loaded with five to 10 colors of lead core line. A monofilament leader ranging from six to 50 feet is attached to the lead core by first removing about two inches of the soft lead wire from the Dacron coating and then tying an overhand knot in the Dacron. The monofilament leader is then tied to the Dacron using a clinch or surgeon knot. The knot in the Dacron acts as a stopper that prevents the monofilament leader from sliding off the end of the lead core.

When fishing this rigging method, the angler lets out the monofilament leader and as much lead core line as necessary to hit bottom or achieve the desired depth level. Normally fished as a flat line, lead core is very effective because the lure is presented a considerable distance behind the boat and the bait runs relatively deep.

SEGMENTED LEAD CORE

A second rigging method known as segmented lead core consists of a monofilament leader, lead core body and monofilament backing. Rigging up segments of lead core begins by spooling 200 yards of monofilament backing onto a levelwind reel. The lead core is then attached to the monofilament backing using the same method described for full lead core and spooled onto the reel. A monofilament leader is attached to the terminal end completing the rig.

Segmented lead core evolved as a method of fishing lead core in combination with in-line planer boards such as the Off Shore Tackle Side-Planer. Using a board significantly increases lure coverage and allows anglers to fish out to the side of the boat and at impressive depths.

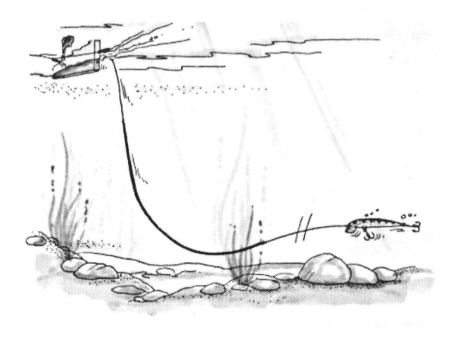

Segmented lead core can be fished with a Side-Planer to increase trolling coverage. Most anglers find that two lines per side is ideal.

When fishing segmented lead core, the board is attached to the monofilament backing and the lure running depth is controlled by how many sections of lead core are used, how much backing is let out and how fast the lures are trolled. This trolling method is most commonly used to reach depths ranging from 30 to 50 feet. It's important to monitor the overall lead length with a line counter reel or you can monitor the backing used with metered fishing line.

The Side-Planer is one of the few boards that are suitable for use with segmented lead core line. Most boards don't track well enough to handle the weight of lead core. The Side-Planer handles three colors with ease and can be used with up to four or five colors of lead core.

Segmented lead core can also be used in combination with catamaran style planer boards. Catamaran boards make it possible to fish more lines and to use longer segments of lead core than practical with in-line boards. The segments of lead core used in this rigging method vary from one color to four or five colors depending on the depth range desired. The most common version consists of three colors of lead core, sandwiched between 200 yards of monofilament backing and 50 feet of leader.

APPLICATIONS

The applications for using lead core are almost without limit. A common tool for reaching suspended walleye, steelhead or land-locked trout, lead core can also be used to present lures near bottom structure for walleye, bass or monster pike. Because of the long leads associated with lead core, the most logical places to incorporate this trolling technique are large areas of open water. Fish that suspend in mid-lake basins or hold tight to bottom on huge flats are prime targets for lead core trolling.

When fishing for suspended fish I recommend using a 40 or 50 foot monofilament leader that helps separate the lure from the lead core line. Lead core is fairly large in diameter and easily spotted in the water. Separating the lure and lead core helps to avoid spooking fish, especially when used in clear waters.

When lead core is used to fish near bottom, it's important to shorten the leader length. Using a shorter lead length makes it easier to determine the exact running depth of trailing lures and maintain better control of these lures.

For structure trolling situations, I usually run a 10 to 20 foot monofilament lead. I also favor a slightly heavier leader material than that used to troll in open water. When structure trolling the chances of hanging bottom greatly increase. It makes sense to use a little heavier leader material in these situations.

When faced with structure situations, it's also important to fish from the bottom up. Let out the leader, lead core and backing until the lure can be felt hitting bottom. Make note of the total lead length, then reel up to be sure the lure hasn't picked up bottom debris on the hooks. Reset the lure using a little shorter lead length so the bait runs just off bottom.

If the bottom is soft, it's often impossible to tell if the lure is hitting the bottom. Check your lines frequently and investigate the hooks for signs of debris that indicate the bait is running too deep.

Despite the long leads associated with lead core trolling, the ratio of hooked to landed fish is excellent. Lead core has little stretch, making for bone piercing hook-sets even at slow trolling speeds.

THE WAYS OF WIRE (Don Parsons)

Wire line trolling picks up where lead core line leaves off. The chief difference between lead core and wire line is that wire line works best when combined with a diving type lure, diving plane or lead weights. Using trolling wire tied directly to lightweight lures such as trolling spoons or spinners offers no advantage over monofilament line or lead core line.

One simple property makes wire line superior in the depth department, diameter. Thin, but exceptionally strong 30 pound test stainless steel multistrand wire is only about .015 thick or about the same thickness as 15 pound test monofilament. When combined with a deep diving crankbait, Dipsy Diver or lead weights, amazing depth levels can be reached trolling wire or what fans of this technique refer to as steel.

WIRE & DEEP WATER TROUT

For years I've used wire line to dredge up lake trout from depths exceeding 100 feet! I use lead weights that vary from one pound to two pounds in weight to achieve the required depth. At the business end a dodger/squid or fly combination is all it takes to strike trout paradise.

The key to this whole system is bumping bottom with the lead weights

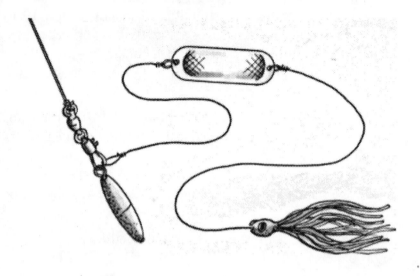

Wire line is often used to fish for deep water fish such as lake trout. This dodger/squid rigging has produced countless trout for the author.

so the trailing dodger and squid flashes back and forth just off bottom. I use three different size lead weights so I can run several lines without fear of tangles.

Tangling lines when you're working with monofilament is a minor setback. If wire lines get tangled, you're simply out of business until all the wire can be cut off the reel and new wire added. Not only is this process a lot of work, but the expense can be even more painful than the lost fishing time.

A simple five rod trolling pattern works best. Using fairly long rods, (8 to 10 feet) I set one line off each side of the boat using a one pound sinker. The long rods help to keep the weights out away from the boat to increase trolling coverage. This fairly light sinker must be let back a considerable distance to make contact with bottom when fishing in 70-100 feet of water.

On each of the back corners of the boat I rig another rod (eight footers are about right) with a pound and half weight. This heavier weight can be kept in contact with bottom using considerably less line out.

Down the middle I'll use a shorter six foot rod with a two pound ball.

This rod fishes at a sharp angle below the boat and straight back avoiding the corner and outside rods in the process.

When these five rods are set properly each weight tunks bottom at a different location and the trailing dodger darts and flashes right in front of bottom hugging trout. If the trout are home, five rods can be a handful for three anglers to manage. It's not uncommon to have two or even three fish on at a time.

The rigging method for this dodger and squid presentation is simple. Level wind reels like the Penn 209 are an excellent choice. Spool up with at least 300 to 400 feet of 30 pound test multistrand stainless wire. Attach a heavy duty snap swivel to the stranded wire by using a couple copper sleeves that are crimped securely.

The lead weights are rigged with a small loop of 50 pound test monofilament so they can easily be attached to the snap swivel. An 18 inch leader of 50 pound monofilament is then clipped to the snap swivel and tied to the dodger. Behind the dodger a squid or fly rigged on 50 pound test monofilament is added. The squid or fly leader should be 8-12 inches long to insure the best snapping action.

For this wire line rig to work properly the sinkers must be bouncing and touching bottom every few feet. If the weight drags on bottom too much wire has been let out, if the weight doesn't touch bottom frequently, the dodger/squid combination will pass over the top of bottom hugging trout and trigger few strikes.

When setting wire lines always let the line out slowly by keeping your thumb on the side of the spool. If you get in a hurry, the line can easily overrun itself and backlash.

Rods for wire line fishing should also be equipped with roller guides and tip top to prevent wear. Wire will chew up and ruin normal guides in no time flat.

WIRE AND DIVERS

The wire line method just described is one of the most productive ways to troll up deep water trout. Wire line has many other trolling applications, but none as popular as using wire line on a diver such as the famous Luhr Jensen Dipsy.

   Trout are one of the primary targets for wire line fishermen, but trolling steel can be effective for many other species.

Combining the Dipsy Diver with wire allows these popular directional divers to achieve much greater depths than possible with monofilament. Using wire on a diver also insures a rock solid hookset that simply isn't possible with monofilament.

Rigging to fish a Dipsy on wire is easy. Spool up a line counter reel with 300-400 feet of 30 pound test braided wire and attach a heavy duty snap swivel on the terminal end using a couple copper sleeves. This snap swivel is attached directly to the Dipsy. Behind the Dipsy a snubber must be installed to prevent fish from tearing the hooks from their mouth. Leaders can range from six to 10 feet depending on rod length.

Heavy duty Dipsy style rods are the best way to fish this trolling hardware. When a fish is hooked, the rod will take an enormous amount of abuse, especially if a large king salmon is at the other end of the line.

A Dipsy diver fished on wire is a popular solution for reaching deep water salmon, trout and steelhead, but walleye anglers also cash in on this technique when fishing large bodies of water such as the Eastern Basin of Lake Erie or the open waters of Lake Huron.

When fishing salmon and trout, a spoon is the most likely lure choice. For walleye, spinners baited with crawlers or stickbaits are the more popular choice.

WIRE AND CRANKBAITS

Wire line is an excellent way to present crankbaits at depths that are significantly greater than possible with monofilament or lead core line. The best baits for trolling with wire are deep diving stickbaits such as the Storm Deep ThunderStick, Bomber 26A or Luhr Jensen Power Dive Minnow. These lures all dive deeper than 30 feet when trolled using monofilament line. On wire the depths achieved can increase by 30, 40 or even 50 percent depending on lead length.

Trolling these diving plugs has become a standard way of tempting deep water walleye in the Central and Eastern Basins of Lake Erie. Anglers combine wire line with catamaran style boards to achieve the best possible depth and the largest trolling coverage.

A typical wire line trolling outfit used on Lake Erie consists of a downrigger style rod equipped with carbide guides and a line counter

99

reel. The reel is loaded with 300-400 feet of 10 to 15 pound test wire. A snap is attached to the end of the wire using a haywire twist or by using copper sleeves crimped tightly shut.

When setting baits the lure is set back the desired lead length then a rubber band is half-hitched over the wire. The rubber band is then buried into the pinch pads of a Off Shore Tackle OR-3 Planer Board Release and sent out to the side via a catamaran style planer board system. Usually three to five lines are fished per side, plus a couple Dipsy lines and a few downrigger lines round out the trolling pattern.

In all honesty, wire line isn't something that beginning trollers are likely to benefit from. It takes a little saavy and practice to handle wire effectively, but in the hands of anglers who know how to get the most from steel, wire line trolling can be a deadly way to reach fish and depths that are out of the reach of lead core line and monofilament.

In the next chapter we'll highlight another form of heavy metal trolling known as Snap Weights. This unique style of trolling is so unique it deserves a whole chapter to explain the many uses and applications.

Sam Anderson is a walleye tournament pro. Don Parsons is a trolling expert with over 40 years experience.

Chapter 11
Snap Weight Trolling
By
Rick "Big Foot" LaCourse

Sooner or later, you're going to add lead to your trolling lines. It's a fact of fishing that weight, in some capacity, is required for many trolling presentations. Usually anglers add weight to achieve a little extra depth, but in some cases the goal is to use enough lead to fish the bottom.

Either way the lead sinkers we put on the line don't catch fish, they simply help position our lures at the desired depth level. In fact, the presense of the sinker is actually a negative that in many cases spooks wary fish and prevents us from better catches. In many trolling situations you're damned if you do and damned if you don't add lead to a trolling line.

Imagine if you could add lead to a trolling line, but instead of using split shots, keel weights, bottom bouncers or other popular trolling weights that are permanently attached to the line, the weight would be attached to a pinch pad line release that could easily be placed on or taken off the line with a simple pinch from your thumb and forefinger. Because the weight is so easy to put on and take off it could be placed anywhere on the line from a few feet ahead of the lure to 100 feet or more up the line.

Instead of the weight always being near the lure where it is likely to spook fish, the trolling sinker could be placed further away from the lure allowing the bait to swim more naturally and still achieve the depth required. Hmmm, now we've stumbled onto a good idea.

Stumbled indeed. The concept for the trolling weight just described was stumbled on by outdoor writer Mark Romanack one day while fishing deep water lake trout with lead drop lines. This crude but effective technique uses a jettison style release to hold a lead ball 25 to 50 feet

101

ahead of a dodger squid or spoon combination. The whole rig is let out until the weight can be felt hitting bottom. When a fish is hooked the jettison release opens up and drops the weight, leaving the angler free to fight the fish without also pulling up a one pound chunk of lead.

The idea of separating the weight and the lure made sense to Romanack, and he could see applications for this technique for walleye, salmon, steelhead and even bass fishing. Romanack also figured that dropping lead into the drink was unnecessary for most trolling situations. "When using weights up to eight ounces, I discovered that reeling in the sinker was no great hardship," comments Romanack. "It didn't take me long to start experimenting with pinch pad line releases with trolling weights attached. The system worked, but the weights kept popping off the line when I'd fight a fish. The concept of snap on trolling weights was sound, but I needed a line clip with a lot stronger spring tension to insure the weight stayed put on the line."

These Snap Weights are color coded to make it easier to determine sizes. Powder paints are the easiest way to color code lead trolling sinkers.

That's when Bruce DeShano of Off Shore Tackle got involved. Romanack asked DeShano if he could build a line release with a super strong spring for his new trolling creation. It didn't take long to determine the ideal spring tension and soon the concept of snap on trolling weights became a new product known as Snap Weights.

The Snap Weight concept caught on quickly with walleye fishermen who troll spinners and stickbaits in open water. It wasn't long before every major player in the walleye tournament circuits was using and recommending Snap Weights.

Gradually Snap Weights found other niche trolling applications for every species from king salmon to striped bass. The uses for Snap Weights continue to amaze Romanack who never dreamed they would become so universal and widely accepted. Several companies have copied the idea and are manufacturing similar products.

The Snap-Weights currently produced by Off Shore Tackle company feature an OR-16 line clip that features a very strong spring tension and a split ring that accepts various size trolling weights. Snap Weights are available in kit form or the components can be purchased separately.

Lead sinkers including 1/2, 3/4, 1, 1.5, 2, 3, 4, 6 and 8 ounce weights are used depending on how deep the angler wants to troll. The smaller size weights are used for suspended fish and the larger weights used to present lures or baits near bottom in up to 50-feet of water.

The same OR-16 line clip used with Snap Weights has become popular with anglers who use in-line boards. The extra tension this clip provides insures that boards like the Side-Planer won't pop off the line while trolling in heavy seas or fighting powerful fish.

THE 50/50 RIGGING METHOD

There are almost as many ways to fish Snap Weights as there are anglers using them. It quickly became obvious that some type of standarized rigging system needed to be developed so anglers could easily share fishing information.

Gary Parsons a two time Pro Walleye Tour Angler-of-the-Year developed a trolling system he calls the 50/50 rigging method. Parsons uses this trolling method to pattern suspended walleye with nightcrawler harnesses, but the basic rigging method can be used with a multitude of

103

The 50/50 rigging method is a common trolling techniques used with Snap Weights. By using different size weights various trolling depths can be achieved.

lures to catch just about any fish that swims.

Parsons' 50/50 spinner system begins with a ball bearing swivel attached to a downrigger style rod rigged with 10 or 12 pound test line. The ball bearing swivel helps eliminate annoying line twist.

A favorite crawler harness is then attached to the ball bearing swivel. Followed by a fat nightcrawler hooked through the nose and about midway in the body.

The baited spinner is then set 50-feet behind the boat. A Daiwa SG27LC line counter reel is used to monitor lead lengths. Next a 1/2, 3/4, 1 or 1.5 ounce Snap-Weight is placed on the line by squeezing open the clip jaws and placing the line midway between the rubber pads.

Once the Snap-Weight is in place, another 50-feet of line is let out and an Off Shore Side-Planer board is added to the line. The Side-Planer is designed to accept the same pinch pad style line clip used with Snap-Weights. Adding an in-line board helps to gain valuable trolling cover-

Snap Weights stay on the line until the angler removes them. The spring tension on the OR-16 clip is strong enough to handle weights up to eight ounces.

age, making the chore of finding and patterning fish much easier.

The 50/50 rigging method puts the spinner 50-feet from the Snap Weight and the Snap Weight 50-feet from the planer board. The in-line board is run from 50 to 150-feet to the side depending on wave conditions.

Start out using several different weights that fish at various depths. Let the fish tell you which weight is best on any given day, Once a certain weight starts producing fish, switch over other lines to the same weight so all the lures are running at the proper depth. Unfortunately, suspended walleyes seldom stay at one depth range for long. I experiment frequently with one line and switch over other lines as necessary.

A dependable sonar unit is a critical part of the Snap-Weight trolling system. When trolling through suspended fish, note the depth range at which most fish are showing up. Later in the day if fish begin to appear at a different depth, you'll know immediately if heavier or lighter Snap-Weights should be used.

Troll at a rather slow .5 to 1.5 mph when fishing spinners. When using the 50/50 system with other lures, such as spoons or crankbaits, faster trolling speeds are often needed to bring out the natural action of these lures.

Anglers who troll with the Snap-Weight and in-line board combination will know the instant they have a strike. The weight of a hooked fish pulls the board sharply back in the water. Those who have never seen an in-line planer board sag from the weight of a nice fish are missing one of the most exciting thrills in trolling.

To land a hooked fish, the board must be reeled in until it's within reach of the boat. The trick is to keep steady pressure on the fish.

Once the board is within reach, remove it by depressing the release. It only takes a split second to remove the board and continue the fight.

When the fish gets within 50-feet of the boat the Snap Weight will appear. The Snap Weight also needs to be removed. Like the planer board, one quick pinch completes the job.

Now the angler simply has to fight the fish to net. It helps to slow down the boat's forward speed at this point to avoid putting any excess

Bruce DeShano of Off Shore Tackle was the first manufacturer to recognize the value of snap-on trolling weights. Since the introduction of this unique product many similar ones have appeared.

pressure on the fish. Once the fish is landed, simply resume trolling at the same speed as before and reset the line.

SNAP WEIGHTS & STRUCTURE FISH

Snap-Weights and the 50/50 rigging system is the perfect combination for suspended fish. A different rigging option is required when fish are located on or near bottom.

When fishing the bottom it's important to have absolute control to prevent lures or the SnapWeights themselves from snagging on bottom. The enitical lead must be shortened to give the angler control. Instead of setting the lure back 50 feet, a lead of 10 to 20 feet works best.

The next step is to use a Snap-Weight that's heavy enough to easily reach bottom. The rule of thumb is to use enough weight so the trailing lures fish at approximately a 45 degree angle from the boat to the bottom. Fishing at a 45 degree angle makes it easier to determine where the

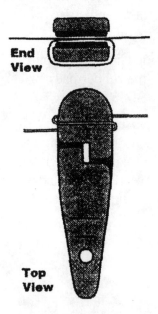

Snap Weights can be used with super braid lines by double wrapping the line through the pinch pad clip twice. Double wrapping prevents these slippery lines from popping out of the rubber pads.

Snap Weight is positioned in relationship to bottom.

Ideally the Snap Weight should be close to but not dragging on the bottom where it churns up silt and can easily become snagged. It takes a little experimenting to get the ideal combination of weight and lead length. Check your lines every few minutes while experimenting to see if the lures come up with bottom debris on the hook. If the lure is hitting bottom either a shorter lead or heavier Snap Weight must be used.

This structure fishing technique isn't as easy to master as the 50/50 rigging method. When using weights up to three ounces in-line boards can be incorporated to gain greater trolling coverage.

Heavier Snap Weights are best fished as flatlines. By spreading out the rods at the back of the boat, four lines can be fished along bottom without fear of tangles. Off Shore Tackle manufactures weights up to eight ounces, but some anglers fish as much as 16 ounces effectively!

Snap Weights were designed for fishing with monofilament lines. If the new super braid lines are used, anglers must take a couple precautions to avoid losing Snap Weights.

When placing the braided line into the pinch pad, wrap the line around the clip jaw and through the rubber pads twice. Double wrapping prevents slippery braided line from popping out of the rubber pads.

As an extra degree of insurance against losing Snap Weights, some anglers add a snap swivel to the split ring and clip the swivel over the line when positioning the Snap Weight. If the weight pops free of the line, the swivel simply slides down the line to the lure, allowing the bait and Snap Weight to be reeled in.

The Snap Weight structure trolling drill is deadly on walleye, trout, bass, pike or any fish that is found near bottom in up to 40 or 50 feet of water. Fishing Snap Weights in water deeper than 50 feet is impractical and a job best handled with downriggers.

In the next chapter tournament pro Gary Parsons outlines his techniques for fishing in-line boards for walleye.

Rick LaCourse is the 1997 PWT champion.

Chapter 12
In-Line Board Tactics
"Walleye Style"
By
Gary Parsons

Fishing is a game that's played by rules that never stop changing. Whenever I look back over the 20 odd years I've spent chasing walleye professionally, I'm startled at the refinements and developments fishing equipment has enjoyed. Even more amazing, I credit a single piece of tackle for jerking the sport of walleye fishing out of the dark ages and thrusting it into the future.

In-line boards like the popular Off Shore Tackle Side-Planer, have helped to shape a new world of walleye fishing opportunities. In recent years, in-line boards have been used to pioneer many new fishing techniques and frontiers.

Prior to the mid 1980's very few anglers trolled for walleye. The most popular angling techniques were based on structure fishing theories supported by writings and literature of the time. Jigging, slip sinker rigs and other methods of fishing live bait were the primary focus.

It wasn't until the development of the in-line planer board that trolling and the concept of open water fishing started to materialize. Only a handful of walleye anglers were experimenting with open water trolling techniques during the early 1980's.

I consider myself to be one of the lucky pioneers that helped to popularize the use of in-line boards for walleye fishing. My first introduction to in-line boards came near my home on Lake Winnebago in central Wisconsin. A shallow lake noted for roaming schools of walleye and sauger, prior to in-line boards the only way to consistently catch these open water fish was by trolling crankbaits on 200 to 300 foot leads.

In theory, the long leads provided spooky fish a few moments to

110

Gary Parsons of Chilton, Wisconsin has been an innovator in the use of in-line boards for walleye fishing. Many of his trolling methods have become widely accepted on the professional walleye tournament trail.

settle down after the boat disturbed them. The elapsed time between the boat passing the fish and the arrival of the lures was enough to fool may of these open water fish into biting the trailing cranks. Crude but effective, long line trolling enjoyed a strong following on Lake Winnebago.

The appearance of in-line boards made a dramatic impact on the Lake Winnebago trolling scene. Long line trollers were quickly converted into board fishermen and open waters of the lake became the proving ground for a piece of fishing equipment known as the in-line planer board.

It wasn't long before in-line board trolling tactics found a home on other waters. Anglers traveling the tournament circuits were among the first to take in-line boards to the Dakotas, Minnesota, Michigan, Ohio and beyond. Currently, anglers across the nation enjoy board fishing opportunities that just a few years ago were unheard of. In fact, board trolling has become the foundation for many of the most productive walleye fishing methods practiced today.

In-line boards get their name because they are designed to attach directly onto the fishing line. When setting an in-line board the angler lets out the desired amount of trolling lead then attaches the board onto the line using a line release or another attachment method. Next the board is placed into the water and more line played off the reel. As the boat trolls along, the board slowly works its way out to the side of the boat, positioning the trailing lures well away from the boat.

When a fish is hooked, the weight of the struggling fish causes the board to pull backwards in the water. Landing the fish requires that the angler reel in both the board and fish until the board can be reached and removed from the line. Once the board is removed from the line, the angler simply fights the fish to net as normal.

One of the common questions I get regarding in-line boards, is what do you do when you're fishing two or more lines per side and a fish is hooked on the outside board? The best way to deal with this situation is to clear the inside line quickly by reeling in the board until it reaches the rod tip. Take the cleared line and place it safely on the opposite side of the boat, then reel in the board with the hooked fish.

Once the fish has been landed, the line that was cleared is placed in the water and sent out to become the outside line. Another option is to

112

In-line boards must be weighted so they ride upright in the water even at slow trolling speeds. For walleye fishing normally two boards are used per side.

freespool the inside board and let it stall in the water while the boat slowly trolls forward. Once the inside line has slid back out of the way, reel in the outside board and fish.

The freespool method works good when using floating/diving style crankbaits, but I wouldn't advise trying it with sinking lures or trolling hardware that sinks.

The first in-line boards produced were hand made of wood, heavy and featured crude line releases or attachment points. Eventually commercially designed models built from lightweight plastic and foam were introduced. Today, the Side-Planer produced by Off Shore Tackle ranks as most popular in-line board among walleye anglers. A number of features have helped make the Side-Planer the board of choice.

A good in-line board must float and be ballasted so it rides upright in the water at rest and at all trolling speeds. Many in-line boards aren't balanced properly. In rough seas or when trolling into the waves, these

113

boards often roll on their side and dive causing major line tangles in the process. The Side-Planer is designed to ride upright in the water no matter what the wave conditions or trolling speed.

The second feature to look for is a board that's easy to put on and take off the line. Remember, when fighting a fish the board must be taken off before the fish can be landed. Obviously the system used to attach the line to the board must be positive, easy to use and fool proof.

The pinch pad style line release pioneered by Off Shore Tackle is the perfect system for attaching in-line boards to fishing line. Attaching the board to the line is as simple as pinching open the spring loaded release and placing the fishing line mid-way between the rubber pads, then closing the release. Removing the board is even easier. A quick pinch between the thumb and index finger is all that's required to free the line.

The Side-Planer comes standard with two OR-14 (black) line releases that meet the needs of most anglers. Many of the pros however substitute the OR-14 with an even stronger spring loaded OR-16 (red) Snap Weight clip. The extra tension of the OR-16 clip guarantees that the board will stay on the line when trolling fast or in heavy seas. The extra spring tension of the OR-16 is also welcome when using braided lines.

For the best performance I recommend using two line attachment points. Attaching the line to the board in two different spots helps it track to the side better and causes the board to be more stable in the water. The two point attachment system also enables the board to better handle deep diving lures or weight systems like Snap Weights, keel sinkers or bottom bouncers.

The Side-Planer is set up to allow anglers two different line attachment options. The first system features two line releases attached to the stainless steel tow arm. One release mounts directly off the tip of the tow arm and the second is mounted along the inside edge.

When the line is attached to both releases on the tow arm, the board tracks with its nose up and the back of the board slightly down in the water. This orientation causes the board to respond quickly when a fish is hooked. The weight of a struggling fish causes the front of the board to pop up out of the water and the whole board to drag backwards. Even a small fish such as a young walleye causes the board to react, making it

114

easy to tell when you've hooked a fish.

This board rigging method works best when trolling at slower speeds and when fishing areas that are plagued with small fish. A second rigging method incorporates a release on the tow arm and one at the back of the board.

Rigged with the line through both the front and rear releases causes the board to run flat on the water. This method is preferred when fishing in heavy seas, trolling at faster speeds or when pulling weights or deep diving lures that have lots of drag in the water.

When fishing the new generation of braided lines, it's necessary to place the line between the rubber pads of the release, then wrap the line around the release and place it between the pads a second time. Double wrapping braided lines insures that these slippery products won't slide through the rubber pads or pop out of the release.

It takes an extra second or two to double wrap braided lines, but this rigging method is the best way to insure the board stays put until the angler is ready to remove it. A lot of line attachment systems have been tried with braided lines, but to date nothing works better than wrapping.

The latest refinement with in-line boards is an unique device called a Tattle Flag. Another Off Shore Tackle innovation, the Tattle Flag is simply a spring loaded flag that goes down when a fish is hooked. This simple addition makes it easy to tell when a small fish is hooked or if a lure is fouled with weeds. Available only as an after market item, Tattle Flags are sold as a kit that contains a flag, two releases, a spring and linkage arm, plus all the necessary hardware to install the flag on Side-Planers.

In-line boards have enjoyed many refinements, but the one feature that makes them so valuable to walleye fishermen hasn't changed. Unlike the larger dual catamaran boards popular on Great Lakes boats, in-line boards can be fished effectively at both slow and fast trolling speeds.

When using boards to fish spinners and other live bait options, it's not uncommon to troll at .5 to .8 MPH. Catamaran boards simply can't function properly at speeds this slow. Because in-line boards can be trolled slowly they have become the obvious choice for fishing a number of slow paced trolling presentations including segmented lead core, Snap Weights, keel sinkers, bottom bouncers and more.

115

I believe that trolling a little slower than the masses is a major reason why I've enjoyed success so often in open water tournaments. Trolling slower keeps the bait in the strike zone of the fish longer and helps to elicit a feeding response, as opposed to the reactionary strike that occurs when a bait is pulled past a fish quickly. Personally, I believe that trolling slowly produces more and bigger walleye most of the time.

At the other end of the spectrum, many anglers believe that in-line boards pulled at a brisk pace trigger strikes that catamaran boards can't. The overall small size of the in-line board causes it to bounce around violently when trolled at speeds upwards of 2.5 MPH. The jerking motion of the board in the water causes the trailing baits to enjoy a stop-and-go action that is deadly on walleye and other game fish species.

Trolling faster is likely to produce best when fishing huge bodies of waters like Lake Erie. On Erie and other large waters, catching large numbers of fish often boils down to simply covering water and contacting as many fish as possible.

In-line boards are mandatory when trolling these large open basins of water. Boards help to spread out lines to achieve a better horizontal coverage of the water. Without the help of boards, finding walleye in open water can be like looking for a needle in a haystack.

Boards also make it practical to fish multiple lines set to run at different depth levels. Now in addition to getting more horizontal coverage, the angler can experiment with vertical coverage of the water.

On a typical day of open water fishing, I'll be using four to six lines depending on how many anglers are aboard. Floating/diving style crankbaits are my first choice for open water trolling. When selecting lures I pick out a couple confidence baits that have worked for me before and use the other lines to experiment with different lures set to run at various depth ranges.

My goal is to cover as much of the water column as possible and let the fish tell me which baits, colors and lead lengths they prefer. About every 15 minutes I change at least one lure in the program as part of the search for the perfect bait.

There's more to open water trolling that putting out a few crankbaits and dragging them around. To be successful you have to keep changing

116

lures and experimenting with lead lengths until the ideal combination is discovered. Once I catch the first fish, I'll switch over another line to duplicate the exact lure, color and lead length that produced the first fish.

It often takes a while to catch the first fish or two, but once the pattern starts to fall into place, the action can get down right feverish. Eventually I'll have all but one of my lines fishing the set up that seems to be producing best on any given day. Being set up to duplicate baits that are working means you'll be purchasing a lot of crankbaits. When I discover a lure that's productive, I often purchase several more identical lures and a few others with different, but similar color patterns.

Since open water fish are often fickle, I like to keep at least one experimental line running all the time. Often I'll set this line to run near the surface. You simply can't depend on your sonar to mark fish that are suspended within the top 10 feet. The only way to know if these fish are present is to set a line and fish for them.

Some of my most memorable catches of walleye have been taken with a few feet of the surface in gin clear water. It just goes to show you, there are no hard and fast rules of open water walleye fishing.

Anyone who's serious about learning the open water trolling game will need to invest in some key equipment. First off, I'd recommend purchasing a small gasoline kicker motor for your boat. A small gasoline motor allows you the flexibility to fish very slow or at fast trolling speeds. The new four stroke models available are amazingly quiet and they squeeze a lot of fishing out of a gallon of fuel.

You'll also need a line counter reel for each of your trolling rods. Line counter reels like the Daiwa SG27LC are an invaluable aid to open water trolling. These reels make it easy to monitor and accurately duplicate lead lengths.

The trick when using line counter reels is to load each reel to capacity with exactly the same pound test line. Spooling up so that each reel has the same amount of line insures that the lead lengths from reel to reel will be consistent.

A third must have item is a GPS unit with a graphics plotter. In open water there are no land marks to guide you. The only practical way to

117

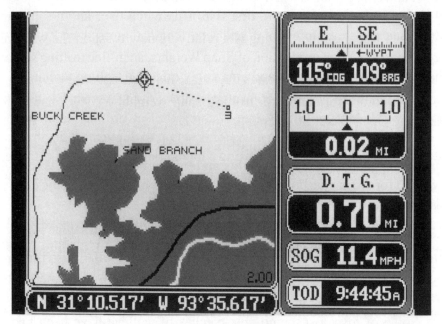

GPS plotters are an invaluable tool for trolling open water. With the help of a graphic plotter anglers can return to productive fishing spots, stay on moving schools of fish and return to port with confidence.

stay on a school of open water fish or to relocate them is with a GPS unit that allows you to save both icons (screen graphics) and waypoints (exact destinations). The Lowrance Global Map 2000 unit I use features five banks of icons and over 200 waypoints. I normally use an icon to mark the location of each fish caught. During the course of a day on the water studying the location of the icons can help you predict the size and shape of the school, plus which direction they are most likely to travel.

I also save at least one waypoint in the area so I can navigate directly back to the spot. While there's no guarantee that open water fish will be in the same area when you return, the valuable waypoints you accumulate over the years become great starting points for future fishing trips. Also the data saved in a GPS unit can be downloaded onto an IBM computer and printed out for future use or passed onto other fishermen.

Many times I'll mark open water fish on my sonar, but they simply won't bite crankbaits. This condition is often associated with cold fronts, changes in weather or if cooler water is pushed into an area. Faced with

118

these conditions the best option is to put away the crankbaits and switch over to spinners.

Open water spinner fishing is a relatively new twist on the walleye trolling scene. The introduction of Snap Weights, an in-line trolling sinker helped to pioneer this new and amazingly effective trolling technique.

For more information on trolling snap weights consult chapter 5, Trolling Open Water Spinners.

The options and combinations available when you combine crankbaits, spinners, Snap Weights and in-line boards are endless. If it weren't for the in-line board, none of these presentations would be nearly as effective.

When it comes to trolling open water walleye, I can't imagine a better way to fish than in-line boards. Without these little boards trolling would be like fishing in the dark ages.

In the next chapter we'll expand our use of in-line boards to include salmon, trout and steelhead fishing. The in-line board trolling techniques outlined by Captain Dave Engel of Best Chance Charters are fast becoming the preferred method for catching these awesome Great Lakes fish.

Gary Parsons is a two time PWT Angler-of-the-Year.

Chapter 13
In-Line Boards For Salmon/Trout
By
Captain Dave Engel

Big boats, big fish and big water is what Great Lakes trolling is all about. Every year anglers travel from around the country to do battle with sizzling king salmon, bruiser browns and tail walking steelhead!

It's fish like these that attract anglers to the Great Lakes. Ironically, catching these monsters often requires a very small piece of fishing equipment known as in-line boards.

In-line planer boards such as the Off Shore Tackle Side-Planer get their name because they attach directly to the fishing line. Each line fished requires a left or right side board. While in-line boards may not look like a big deal, these little fishing tools are often the key to catching salmon, steelhead, brown trout and even lakers when these species are located near the surface.

Any time the surface temperature is less than 55 degrees, salmon and trout are likely to be feeding near the top. Most years that means that excellent fishing can be enjoyed with in-line boards during the months of April, May, June, October and November.

How close to the top are these fish located? In many cases the fins of steelhead and other Great Lakes trophies can be spotted sticking out of the surface film! Most of the fish will be located within the top 30 feet, even though the water may be several hundred feet deep.

Early and late in the year, all the Great Lakes species can be found close to shore. Anglers fishing from small and big boats alike share in the action. As spring wains into summer, the water along the beaches warms beyond the 55 degree mark and fish move off shore where they can find cooler water. In some cases anglers run 20-25 miles to locate

120

Captain Dave Engel is a successful Great Lakes troller. His in-line board trolling strategy is considered by many to be the ultimate fishing method for surface steelhead.

the ideal fishing conditions.

Obviously fishing this far from shore requires a sea worthy boat capable of making long comfortable runs. The boat must also be equipped with a navigation system such as a GPS unit and a high quality VHF marine radio.

All this equipment may seem like overkill, but the quality of fishing is worth every penny invested in boats, motors and accessories. The average day on the water produces 10 fish and many days anglers are treated to 20 or more hook-ups!

Until you've experienced a raging steelhead jumping or a powerful king smoking the reel drag you can't appreciate the excitement these fish generate. The Great Lakes trolling bite is big game fishing at its finest.

The in-line boards that make this exciting sport possible aren't exactly new items on the trolling scene. Anglers have been using the Off Shore Tackle Side-Planer and other in-line boards for many years.

Most anglers know that in-line planer boards help spread out the trolling coverage, but what many don't understand is that these fishing tools can actually improve the action of trailing baits. When an in-line board is trolled it jerks and darts when pulled through the waves. Because the board is attached directly to the fishing line, the darting action of the board also influences the swimming action of baits.

Saying that in-line boards change the action of lures may not be entirely accurate. What's actually happening is that the constant lure action associated with trolling is being momentarily interrupted by the movement of the planer board.

How important is this interruption of lure action? According to many professional anglers, charter captains and serious anglers, the benefit to lure action in-line boards provide is invaluable. "It's not so much the change in lure action that triggers strikes, but rather the hesitation that occurs when a bait slows down or stops for a brief second that's irresistible to trout and salmon," says Bill Bale of Best Chance Charters.

The captains at Best Chance Charters prefer the Off Shore Tackle Side-Planer board, but not the way the board comes in the package. "We modify the board considerably, says Bale to meet our needs." "The first

122

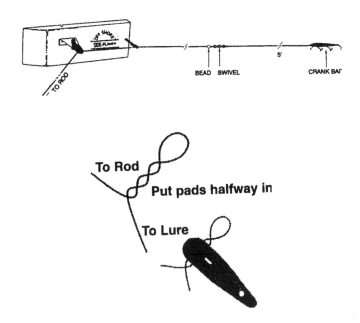

In-line boards are ideal for steelhead trolling when the fish are located near the surface. This illustration shows how to rig for success.

step is to remove the flag. Walleye anglers need the flag to help determine strikes, but when fishing for steelhead or other Great Lakes fish the flag is just extra weight."

"Next we remove the lead ballast weight and clip away about 1/3 of the lead weight with a pair of side cutters," adds Bale. "Making the board a little lighter causes it to toss around a little more in the waves and makes it easier to reel in when fish are hooked or when changing lures."

The next step is to remove the release mounted at the back of the board and replace it with a large snap swivel. The snap swivel is clipped over the line and allows the angler to trip the board and let it slide down when fighting a fish.

"The final modification is to replace the model OR-14 (black) release that comes with the board with a heavy tension (red) OR-16 Snap Weight clip," explains Bale. "The heavier tension of this line clip makes it possible to troll at high speeds or when making turns without the boards

123

accidentally tripping."

These simple modifications take about five minutes and enable the Side-Planer to function flawlessly as a salmon and steelhead board. Because Side-Planer boards are a little larger than other in-line skis, they track to the side better making it easier to run several lines per side. Also the larger size handles rough water better, a fact of fishing in big water.

Rods used for fishing in-line boards need to have enough backbone to handle the in-line board and heavy fish, yet offer a forgiving action that acts as a shock absorber when fighting powerful fish. Downrigger rods tend to make ideal planer board rods. Look for models made from fiberglass or fiberglass/graphite composites that are rated to handle 10-20 pound test line. The more guides these rods have the better and look for handles made from foam instead of cork. Cork tends to wear out quickly when subjected to the wear and tear rod holders dish out.

For most Great Lakes fishing a premium monofilament in the 17 to 20 pound test category is ideal.

Ball bearing swivels are another small but essential trolling item. If spoons are to be used a quality ball bearing swivel must be attached to the terminal end to achieve the maximum action without line twist. A simple cross-loc snap should be used for lines that will receive stickbaits and diving cranks.

On about one third of the lines a barrel swivel is tied in-line about six feet ahead of the lure with a 1/2 or 3/4 ounce egg sinker threaded onto the line ahead of the swivel. This lead weight helps spoons run a foot or two deeper and also stops the board from sliding all the way down to the fish.

Lines that will be used to pull stickbaits or diving cranks are equipped with a Speedo bead threaded onto the line about six foot in front of the lure to stop the board. The Speedo bead can be installed in seconds without having to cut the line and it acts to stop the board from sliding down to the fish.

A few additional lines are rigged with a barrel swivel tied in-line about six feet ahead of the lure. These lines are used with Snap Weight in-line trolling sinkers to achieve a little extra depth than is practical with a slip sinker rig.

124

In-line boards are commonly used to present stickbaits like these. Spoons and diving crankbaits can also be used in combination with in-line boards.

125

Snap Weights are simply an OR-16 clip with a split ring that accepts trolling weights up to eight ounces. For board trolling weights ranging from 1/2 to three ounces are attached directly onto the line 25 to 50 feet ahead of the lure. The Snap Weight stays on the line until the angler reels it up and removes it during the fight. The whole process of putting on and taking off Snap Weights takes a matter of seconds.

When it's time to set all these lines the process goes amazingly smooth. Lines that are set without Snap Weights are set 50-100 feet behind the boat and the planer board attached to the line.

"The best way we've found to attach an in-line board to monofilament is to loop the line around your finger and twist it half a dozen times, then position the twisted line in the planer board release," explains Bale. "This method insures that the board will hold securely on the line until a fish strikes. Most fish pull the twisted line free of the release instantly, but with smaller fish we often have to trip the board by popping the rod tip sharply."

Using this ingenious trip and slide down rigging method up to five or six boards can be fished per side. On a calm day the outside lines are often set to run out 150 feet from the boat. During rougher conditions the boards can be run effectively much closer to the boat.

Lines that are to be fished with Snap Weights get a slightly different treatment. The desired spoon or body bait is let back 25 to 50 feet and then a Snap Weight is attached to the line. Next the Snap Weight is let back another 25 to 50 feet, the in-line board attached and the whole shooting match let out to the side 50 or more feet.

Lines rigged with Snap Weights become the out and down lines, fishing slightly deeper than clean lines rigged with spoons or body baits. Snap Weights can be used effectively with spoons, stickbaits or diving crankbaits to achieve a multitude of fishing depth ranges.

A handful of trusted lures have surfaced as the best choices for this deadly trolling system. Favorite stickbaits include the Storm ThunderStick and Jr. ThunderStick, Bagley Bang-O-Lure and Rapala Husky Jerk. Productive floating/diving style cranks include the Storm Rattlin' Thin Fin, Wiggle Wart and Rattle Tot, plus the Luhr Jensen Hot Shot and Producers Willy's Worm. The best colors are usually fluorescent red, firetiger,

King salmon like this are frequent victims of in-line board trolling tactics. This fish taken by John Campbell was caught in Lake Michigan.

chartreuse and other bright shades.

The top producing trolling spoons are the Wolverine Silver Streak, Pro Spoon, Dreamweaver and Stinger. Productive colors include silver with orange, silver/orange/green, watermelon, gold/orange and gold/orange/green.

The Great Lakes offer a wealth of trolling opportunities. When most anglers think of these deep, clear water lakes they conjure up images of downriggers and fish taken 60, 70 or 80 feet below the surface. This image may only be half true. The fastest fishing action often takes place in the top 30. Once you've made a commitment to fish the surface, and purchased a few in-line boards the rest is down hill. After all, catching fish isn't difficult, it's knowing where to look that's the hard part.

In-line boards are the rage these days, but the dual catamaran style board is still the king of board trolling. The next chapter outlines double skis and provides tips that will help anglers catch just about anything that swims.

Dave Engel is a charter captain, tournament pro, and trolling specialist.

Lake trout are also surface feeders during the cool water periods.

Chapter 14
Catamaran Style Boards
By
Captain Al Lesh

Catamaran boards exemplify the spirit of trolling more than just about any other form of fishing. Perhaps it's the fact that catamaran boards are one of the most publicized forms of trolling, or that the boards and mast themselves are simply more visible and obvious to other anglers. Whatever the reason, dual boards have carved out a niche in the trolling scene that can't be denied.

The Great Lakes is one such arena. Catamaran style boards dominate the sprawling waters of Lakes Michigan, Huron, Superior, Erie and Ontario. Almost everything that swims in these waters including walleye, salmon, steelhead, brown trout, lake trout, musky, northern pike and even small mouth bass are frequent victims of these universal trolling tools.

Other strong holds for catamaran boards include the huge reservoirs of the western states. It's here that walleye, salmon and several different species of trout fall prey to board trolling tactics.

In the nation's midsection and deep south, catamaran boards find a home with striper fishermen who often troll up fish topping 30 pounds! Catamaran boards are also at home in salt water. The list of salt water species catamaran boards routinely produce is too large to list.

Collectively, catamaran boards are the most popular and wide spread form of board trolling. The introduction of the in-line board has nibbled away at the catamaran board market, but the overall impact has been minor. The fact remains that dual boards are simply better suited to many trolling applications.

THE UPS & DOWNS OF CATAMARAN BOARDS

129

Captain Al Lesh is an advocate of dual planer boards. Anglers who fish large boats prefer these larger skis because they can run numerous lines with ease.

Catamaran Style Boards

Like any form of fishing, trolling with catamaran boards has both advantages and disadvantages. The primary disadvantage of fishing dual boards is the rather expensive bottom line. A good set of dual skis start at around $100.00, a mast and retrieval system costs another $150.00 and a couple dozen quality line releases will set an angler back around $50.00.

Anglers trying to save a buck have been building home-made versions of dual skis, masts and even line releases almost as long as these products have been on the market. The problem with these home-made gadgets is they are usually just that gadgets that simply don't meet the task at hand.

Many of the complaints about board trolling and equipment failures can be traced to home-made fishing tackle. Designing and building a catamaran board that functions flawlessly is a little more complicated that chopping off two pine boards and hooking them together with threaded rod. Masts, line retrieval systems and even something as simple looking as a planer board release simply can't be duplicated at home.

Anglers are far better off to purchase a commercially designed and built catamaran system than to cobble around with home-made versions. Riviera Downriggers produces one of the widest assortments of quality and affordable catamaran trolling equipment on the market. The Dual Collapsible Planer Board is bright yellow for easy visibility, folds for convenient storage and can be used on either side of the boat. This trusted board also features an adjustable tow arm that allows the angler to match the board to the trolling conditions.

In addition Riviera also produces two planer board masts. The standard mast features a reinforced fiberglass boom that's the most durable in the industry. Equipped with two lexan reels that pick up two feet of planer line per handle revolution, the mast comes completely assembled and includes required pulleys, planer board line and a termination kit.

A new product the Kachman/Riviera Automatic Planer Board Mast does something no other mast system can do. A pair of spring loaded reels automatically lets out and retrieves the planer board line when setting and picking up boards. The angler simply needs to choose the distance the boards will fish away from the boat before going fishing and wrap the line around a convenient stop.

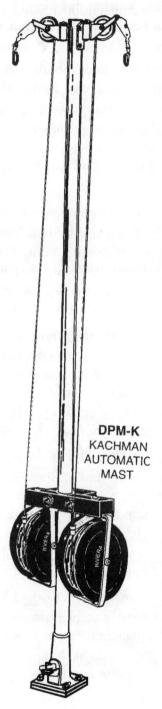

DPM-K
KACHMAN
AUTOMATIC
MAST

In addition to being easier to set and pickup boards, the automatic reel system picks up slack line when making turns than allows the board to work its way back out to the pre-set position when the boat straightens out. With the Riviera/Kachman Automatic Planer Mast, catamaran skis can be mounted to any boat, even those with limited access to the bow.

While a dual planer board system requires a substantial investment, quality equipment will provide a lifetime of faithful service. All Riviera products are made in the U.S.A. and service is available at the manufacturing plant in Port Austin, Michigan.

Turning to the advantages, dual boards have many features that make them the ideal choice for board trolling. Big boards by their very nature are superior when trolling in rough seas. A fact of fishing on many large and wind swept waters, catamaran style boards plow through rough water and resist diving better than even the highest quality in-line boards.

The size of dual boards also makes them the logical choice when trolling large or deep diving lures. Big lures like those commonly used by musky trollers or super deep diving crankbaits have too much drag in the water to fish effectively with in-line boards. The same is true of other trolling hardware such as diving planers,

The Kachman/Riviera Automatic Mast is one of the most simple and unique aids for planer fishing ever developed..

dodgers, gang spinners, lead core line, in-line weights and wire line. All of these trolling accessories and more can be fished effectively using catamaran style boards.

When it's important to run large numbers of lines, nothing tops a catamaran board system. Many charter captains and other advocates of big boards routinely fish five or six lines per side. Fishing so many lines makes it easier to find and pattern fish by offering a wide variety of baits and lure colors. Fishing so many lines also allows baits to be positioned at a wide variety of depths, further helping to locate and pattern fish.

Another advantage of catamaran style boards is they can be used to fish for a wide assortment of game fish by making only minor changes. The line releases used with catamaran boards feature different tension settings designed for different size fish and pound test lines. By simply making this simple equipment adjustment, catamaran boards can be used to catch almost anything that swims.

CHOOSING LINE RELEASES

It's important to select a line release that offers the proper tension setting. If the tension is too light, anglers will be plagued with false releases. If the tension is too tight, a fish can't trip the release once hooked and could ultimately break the line.

Quality pinch pad line releases are available to suit just about any board trolling situation. The leading manufacturer of planer board releases is Off Shore Tackle, LLC. The most copied family of releases on the market, it seems that just about everyone favors the Off Shore Tackle pinch pad design.

Part of the reason the Off Shore release has become so popular is because each of their many designs were engineered and built by anglers for anglers. "Building a quality line release is no simple task," admits Bruce DeShano, owner of Off Shore Tackle. "For a release to function properly it must hold the line securely yet give up its grip on the line at precisely the right moment. It must also have enough tension to insure a good hookset, and never damage or weaken the line."

Building all these features into a line release proved a monumental task. "It has taken years of designing and countless hours of prototyping to come up with the releases we currently sell," adds DeShano. "All our

133

Many of Off Shore Tackle's smaller line releases feature an adjustable spring tension. The tension in larger size releases can be adjusted by how deeply the fishing line is placed into the rubber pads.

releases are made in the U.S.A., and many feature adjustable tension settings. One of our releases will meet any sportfishing need from the Great Lakes to the Gulf of Mexico."

When fishing catamaran boards for small to medium sized fish such as walleye, bass or spring browns, the OR-10 or OR-14 releases are a good choice. When the target fish are a little larger, the OR-3 features a larger pad diameter and a little more tension. This release is the favorite of Great Lakes trout, salmon and steelhead fishermen. It also is popular for anglers who fish for deep water walleye or for stripers.

For special trolling situations such as musky and salt water, the heavy tension of the OR-8 is required. This release features a double spring to insure that large fish or those with a bony mouth are hooked.

Anglers looking for one release to cover all or most of their trolling needs are best equipped with the OR-3. This release can be set light for fish such as walleye, by simply placing the line near the edge of the pad. For bigger fish bury the line deeper into the rubber pads.

The basic strategy used to catch fish with catamaran boards remains

134

the same no matter what species is being targeted. The lures and releases used make the difference.

BOARD TRICKS

There are a few tricks that make board fishing easier and more effective. One of the tricks seasoned board trollers use to prevent line tangles is to space out their rod holders near the back of the boat and to tilt each rod at a slightly lower angle to the water. The rod closest to the bow is positioned in the rod holder pointing almost straight up and is attached to the outside bait or lure fished closest to the board. Each new line set is positioned in the rod holder with the tip tilted a few degrees closer to the water. The rod connected to the inside line points almost straight out from the side of the boat.

It's best to space out each line 10 to 20 feet apart to prevent the lures from tangling one another. It's also a good ideal to avoid lures that wander a lot if lots of lines are set per side. Baits like the Storm Hot 'n Tot are excellent fish getters, but if spaced too close together the baits often swim together and fouled one another. When fishing the maximum number of lines per side, be sure to select lures that track straight.

Another simple trick that makes setting lines with catamaran style boards easier is to coat the planer board line with a little bow string wax. Waxing the line allows the releases to slide along the tether line smoothly and more quickly. To keep everything moving along smoothly, wax the line two or three times a year.

Anglers who troll using the new super braid lines have no doubt discovered that these lines don't function well in pinch pad style planer board releases. A trick that works well when using braided lines is to half hitch a rubber band onto the braided line at the point the release would attach. Break the rubber band and then place it between the pads of the release.

This simple solution to trolling with braided lines also works well when trolling wire or lead core line. Another benefit of this system is the rubber band also marks the lead length, making easy to reset the line and duplicate leads that produce fish.

Many anglers troll with their boards out 100 to 150 feet to the side of the boat. While the boards function fine out this far, it makes it tougher

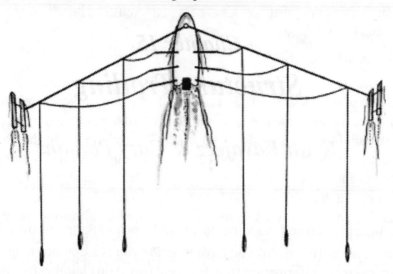

A dual board planer system is best when running three or more lines per side. Most anglers run the boards out to the side 70-80 feet. Dependable pinch pad line releases are required to make this system work. For salmon and trout fishing the Off Shore OR-3 is recommended. For smaller fish such as walleye or brown trout most anglers prefer the OR-10 light tension release.

to turn tightly without tangling lines. Running the boards 75 to 100 feet out allows the boat to be turned rather sharp, which is a big advantage when trying to stay on a small school of fish.

The users of catamaran boards are a loyal lot. Once you've mastered this fishing technique, it's hard to imagine fishing any other type of board. While most of the big ski systems sold each year end up on larger boats, a catamaran system can be installed and used effectively on just about anything that floats.

In the next chapter three of the nation's top walleye professionals discuss the topic of structure trolling. The techniques outlined are deadly on walleye, but they are just as effective for many other bottom hugging species from bass to northern pike.

Chapter 15
Structure Trolling
By
Keith Kavajecz & Gary Parsons

Imagine yourself standing on a boat launch looking out over a lake you've never fished. All you have to guide you is a contour map of the lake and some information from the local bait shop claiming this fishery offers lots of good pike, bass and walleye action. Where do you begin?

The bottom is always a good place to start searching for fish when learning new water. Sure, a lot of fish will suspend to take advantage of free swimming forage species, but in most waters, most of the time, bass, pike, walleye and other species are more likely to be found on or near the bottom.

Making a commitment to fish the bottom is the first step. The second step is identifying specific angling tactics that are efficient at eliminating the vast amounts of unproductive water you'll encounter. Unfortunately, many structure fishing techniques such as jig casting, slip sinker rigging and wind drifting eat up the clock to quickly to be considered serious fish finding methods.

Trolling is the only logical way to cover water quickly. When it comes to fishing bottom structure, two trolling techniques known as jig trolling, and crankbait contour trolling shine brightest. Each one of these tactics covers water quickly and patterns active fish. Once fish are located, a slower paced presentation may well be the best way to catch the largest numbers of fish.

137

Keith Kavajecz caught this monster walleye by using a little known structure fishing technique called jig trolling.

138

JIG TROLLING
(Keith Kavajecz)

The concept of trolling jigs is as foreign to most anglers as live bait is to a bass fisherman. Jigs are casted, fished vertical, drifted, dragged, hopped, ripped and fished a dozen other ways, so why not troll them?

Actually the concept of jig trolling came to me and my fishing partner Gary Parsons as a hybrid of two different jigging techniques. We were fishing the Fort Peck Reservoir in Eastern Montana where a friend and fellow tournament angler Mike Kohler was catching some fish using a method known as rip jigging. In rip jigging the angler drags the jig well behind the boat and jerks it off bottom and allows the bait to settle back down on a slack line. An aggressive fishing method, rip jigging moves so fast that it doesn't allow the angler much control of the jig once it's jerked off bottom.

Avid vertical jiggers, Gary and I started to ponder the idea of mixing the finer points of vertical jigging with the rip jigging technique Kohler was using. In vertical jigging we control both the lift and fall of the jig and also have the advantage of fishing two rods. The problem with vertical jigging is it moves along too slowly to be effective at finding fish.

By combining rip jigging with vertical jigging a hybrid technique we call jig trolling evolved. Here's how the system works.

Jig trolling is a technique that produces best when two anglers work together as a team. The angler at the front of the boat controls an electric motor, sets the trolling speed and keeps the boat moving along a specific depth contour. This angler also selects two fairly heavy jigs, usually 3/8 ounce, and establishes a speed at which these jigs can be fished at roughly a 45 degree angle to bottom without losing feel of the bottom.

The angler in the back of the boat also fishes two rods, but with lighter 1/8 or 1/4 ounce jigs. In order to maintain contact with bottom these jigs must be fished further behind the boat.

Jig trolling accomplishes a lot of important points. Most importantly the boat is moving along a specific depth contour and searching for fish. Secondly, the jigs can be fished in a controlled manner, allowing the angler to lift and drop them using a variety of actions or fish triggering

139

Jig trolling is a good way to quickly work out bottom contours. It's best to work as a team with the angler in the bow controlling the boat and fishing 3/8 ounce jigs. The angler in the back of the boat uses lighter 1/4 ounce jigs and lets his lures drag back behind the boat.

techniques. Jig trolling also allows the anglers to fish two rods each, maximizing the number of baits in the strike zone. In addition a jig troller can experiment with different color jigs, live baits or grub bodies while fishing. And lastly, jig trolling offers the fish two different presentations at the same time.

Active fish are likely to bite the first presentation that passes them. The angler fishing in the front of the boat is going to catch most of the active fish. The angler fishing in the back of the boat picks off the neutral or negative fish, or those active fish missed by the front angler.

Experimenting with different jigging actions helps to determine which method will trigger more bites. One of the most productive jigging strokes is for the front angler to simply lift the jig a little off bottom and wait for a two count before slowly dropping the bait back to bottom. When using this technique the bite is usually felt as a sensation of weight when you lift the jig or as a tick on the line when the jig is dropping back.

The angler in the back of the boat uses a pop and flutter style action that lifts the jig sharply off bottom and allows it to free fall back to bottom. When using this technique most of the strikes are detected when lifting the jig off bottom.

I also experiment a lot with different live baits and grub bodies. For walleye fishing we typically use a small minnow, leech or half a nightcrawler as bait. Bass and pike fishermen may find that a larger minnow or simply a jig dressed with a grub body is the best bait option.

When fishing a minnow I'd suggest using a stinger hook. Because jig trolling is a technique that moves along quickly, a lot of short bites are experienced. A stinger hook helps to catch fish that didn't get the minnow completely in their mouth.

Stingers work very well on minnows, but you simply can't sting a nightcrawler or a leech. These live baits ball up on the stinger hook making for a very unappealing live bait package.

When small fish such as perch or bluegill become a problem, try switching form a live bait to a scented soft plastic worm such as the Berkley Power Jig Worm. This bait has an action similar to a live crawler, but it stays on the hook much better than the real thing.

When using soft plastics you don't have to worry about the hook being baited. Plastics are especially helpful when you feel a bite and miss the fish. Simply drop the bait back down and most times the fish will hit it again. With live bait, if you miss the fish, the bait is usually ripped off and the fish triggering effects of the lure lost.

WHERE TO JIG TROLL

Jig trolling is an excellent technique for covering shorelines in natural lakes and reservoirs. Simply pick a depth contour and follow that depth religiously. If necessary you can move up shallow or out a little deeper to continue the search.

Depending on water clarity, jig trolling works best in water from six to about 20 feet deep. Below 20 feet other techniques such as bottom bouncers or crankbaits are more efficient. The most productive depth zones tend to be from eight to 15 feet.

It's important to remember that jig trolling is a fish finding technique. Once fish are located other methods may be more efficient at catching

141

them, especially if the fish are concentrated on specific spots where an angler could cast a jig or crankbait directly into the school.

It may help some anglers to think of jig trolling as a moving cast. The action of the jigs is similar to that used when casting jigs. The major difference is the boat is used to pick up the slack and keep the presentation moving.

JIG TROLLING ESSENTIALS

A number of pieces of equipment can make jig trolling a more enjoyable and productive experience. A powerful electric motor with a variable speed control and constant on switch is essential. Set the boat trolling speed as discussed before and switch the electric motor into the constant on position.

Because an electric motor has a 360 degree turning radius it's easier to stay on winding bottom contours with an electric motor as opposed to a gasoline kicker motor. An auto-pilot style electric motor is a great aid for this style of fishing because it helps keep the boat on course when the angler pauses to bait a hook or fight a fish.

Another tool anglers may want to consider is using braided lines like FireLine. The thin diameter and low stretch characteristics of this line allow the angler to fish faster, while maintaining contact with bottom. Also, every little tick or bump on the line will be felt by the angler, making it easier to feel bites. The 10 pound test product is the diameter of four pound test line and the six pound test is the diameter of two pound test monofilament.

Quality graphite rods are also a must for jig trolling. The angler in the front of the boat will need a set of seven foot medium action triggersticks with matching baitcasting reels. The extra rod length helps to keep the line away from the boat where it can't tangle with the prop, transducers or other objects.

The angler fishing in the back of the boat is best equipped with a set of five foot-nine inch spinning rods and a lightweight spinning reel. These rods need to be extra sensitive because most of the time the jigs will be positioned well away from the boat.

Jig trolling is a refined style of structure fishing that's deadly on walleye, bass, pike or just about any species of fish that frequently hugs the bottom.

Crankbaits are an overlooked tool for fishing bottom structure. This trolling technique can be used to catch walleye, bass, pike and many other species.

CONTOUR TROLLING CRANKBAITS
(Gary Parsons)

Make no mistake, the fastest way to fish bottom structure is with a crankbait. Add in the fact that crankbaits are attractive to a wide variety of species, plus they often produce the biggest fish and it's easy to see why structure or contour trolling cranks is a popular and productive fish finding technique.

While contour trolling is a common angling technique, not many anglers understand the dynamics that go into effective structure trolling. The biggest mistake anglers make when contour trolling is to position the boat on structure. It's not the location of the boat, but rather the lures that are trailing behind the boat that's important.

When a boat follows a depth contour, the trailing bait doesn't always follow the path of the boat. In fact if the contour has a lot of cups, inside turns, bends and protruding points, these key fish attracting spots may be missed entirely if the boat follows the contour.

Imagine your boat moving along and sticking tightly to a specific break line with a crankbait set to run just off bottom. When the bottom contour suddenly takes a rather sharp turn towards deeper water, the boat is turned to stay at the same depth range. When the boat turns sharply to stay on course, the trailing crankbait is actually forced to swing inside to shallower water, missing the cup completely and usually fouling on weeds or bottom debris.

In order to place the crankbait into the cup and waiting fish, the boat must be positioned to run inside the depth contour just before reaching the cup, then swung at a 90 degree angle towards deeper water that in turn sweeps the baits into the cup.

If the tip of a point is the target, the boat must be turned outside 90 degrees just before it reaches the point then swung back to pass slightly off the tip of the point so the trailing lures contact the tip of the point.

The key to structure trolling with crankbaits is to concentrate on where your baits are running and to position the boat so trailing lures hit the areas most likely to harbor fish. Since it's not practical to be changing lead lengths while trolling, the boat must be used to keep the lures running at or near a specific depth range.

144

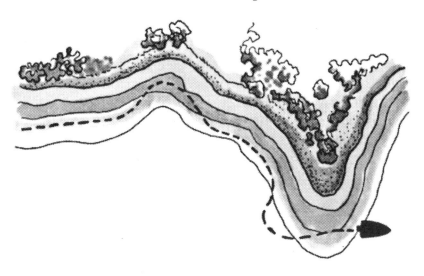

Structure trolling with crankbaits requires that the angler anticipate changes in the contour before the lures reach them. The key is to sweep lures into specific areas such as an inside turn or the tip of a point.

It's also important to know how to manipulate the diving depth of various floating/diving style crankbaits. The primary factors that control how deep a crankbait will dive are line diameter and lead length.

Small diameter lines have less drag in the water and allow crankbaits to reach maximum depths. For contour trolling super thin lines like FireLine are a good choice. Because lures dive deeper on this super thin braided line, shorter and easier to control leads can be use. Also, using braided lines allows crankbaits to be fished deeper than possible with monofilament lines, allowing cranks to be fished on structure out to 30, 40 or even 50 feet of water if necessary.

Trolling leads are the second factor that dictates crankbait running depth. When fishing relatively short leads the baits follow the contour the boat is traveling rather closely. However, when longer leads are needed to achieve the proper lure depth, the boat must be manipulated to accurately swing lures into cups, across points and key fish concentration centers.

All of these trolling chores are best accomplished with a small gasoline outboard motor. Motors in the 9.9 to 25 horsepower range are ideally

145

suited to providing both a quiet and efficient means of power.

TIPS FOR SETTING AND CHOOSING LURES

Water clarity determines how close to bottom trailing cranks should be positioned. If the water is murky, it's important to position the bait within a foot of bottom. In clear water, fish can easily see baits and will chase them much further off bottom. In clear water the angler enjoys the flexibility of positioning baits two or three feet off bottom.

When setting lures I let out line until I can feel the bait hitting bottom then shorten the lead slightly so the bait runs just off bottom. A line counter reel is invaluable for determining the ideal lead lengths and duplicating them once fish are caught.

The best lures tend to be baits that closely resemble the natural forage species available. In natural lakes where spottail or emerald shiners are the most common forage, slender minnow shaped baits are the best choice. In reservoirs where gizzard or threadfin shad are abundant lures with a shad shaped profile are good choices.

When picking colors, I like to stay with natural shades that do a good job of imitating available forages. Color choices such as Tennessee Shad do a good job of duplicating the color range of shad or other minnows. Firetiger that's primarily green and yellow matches nicely with another common forage fish the yellow perch.

In dark, dirty or stained waters, brightly colored baits are more visible and will almost certainly produce the best action. In clear water the closer a lure matches natural forages the better it is likely to work.

INCORPORATING BOARDS WITH CONTOUR TROLLING

In-line planer boards can be useful when trolling contours with crankbaits in a number of ways. I frequently use an in-line board when structure trolling in relatively shallow water. The board does an excellent job of positioning the trailing lure away from the noise and water disturbance the boat creates.

If the fish are located in less than six feet of water, boards may be the only way to avoid spooking them. Boards can also be handy for fishing an outside line that runs in deep water adjacent to the primary contour you're focusing on.

I frequently encounter suspended fish when I'm structure trolling. Most of the time these fish are relating to a dominate feature, such as a point that juts out into deep water. Pods of fish usually suspend at roughly the level of the top of the structure, but out a little ways in open water. These fish suspended off the tip of a point may be feeding on a suspended forage base, or simply resting until conditions favor a move up onto the structure.

Running that outside board line with a crankbait set for suspended fish has saved a lot of otherwise tough fishing days. I encounter this phenomenon mostly on large reservoirs that have a population of smelt, alewives, or shad that suspend in the water column, but the pattern also exists in most Great Lakes waters and some large natural lakes with free roaming forage species such as ciscoes or young-of-the-year drum.

GPS AND STRUCTURE TROLLING

A GPS unit with a plotter is invaluable for this type of structure fishing. Keeping in mind that structure trolling is used primarily to locate fish, it follows that a GPS unit is handy for marking the locations of fish that mark on the graph, landed fish or simply spots along the structure that appear to have features fish look for such as schools of bait, cups, bends or points.

When contour trolling I often follow a section of shoreline for two miles or more. As I'm working my way along, I'll save important features using an icon or graphic that appears on the plotter screen. Once I've completed a trolling run, I can then go back and work these key features using a different technique more suited to this particular location such as casting a jig or crankbait.

OTHER TIPS

It's not practical to fish bottom contours using more than three lines. I normally opt for a board line to fish the inside, a flat line to fish the contour the boat is following and an outside board line set to run off bottom for suspended fish.

If you're doing it correctly structure trolling is going to claim some of your crankbaits. Because you'll be snagging bottom and going back to free lines occasionally, it makes sense to keep the total number of lines to a minimum. Also, structure trolling requires the angler to reel in and check his lines frequently to make sure they haven't picked up leaves, pieces of weeds or other bottom debris.

It also helps to structure troll with the wind at your back whenever possible. It's tough enough to accurately position the boat without having to deal with a wind that's constantly blowing the boat off course.

Developing a sense for contour trolling takes a little practice, but the rewards are more than worth the effort. An excellent way to locate bottom loving fish, crankbaits and structure are natural partners in the hands of a troller who knows how to structure troll.

In the next chapter the focus turns to bottom bouncers, another excellent method for fishing bottom structure.

*Gary Parsons and Keith Kavajecz are walleye tournament pros and brother-in-laws.

Chapter 16
Trolling With Bottom Bouncers
By
Mike McClelland

If you haven't fished a bottom bouncer before, I wouldn't be surprised. Although these structure fishing aids are very popular in the my home state of South Dakota, their acceptance in the rest of the fishing world hasn't been universal. Outside of a few midwestern states known for walleye fishing, the virtues of bottom bouncers aren't widely known.

It's a shame that bottom bouncers aren't working their magic from coast to coast. Not only are these trolling weights one of the best ways to catch walleye, they also work equally well on any species of fish that is often found near bottom real estate.

Once you've tried one of these strange looking wire sinkers, you'll be wondering how you ever fished on or near the bottom without them. While I wouldn't call a bottom bouncer a finesse form of fishing, I've seen these rigs charm fish into biting more times than I can remember.

For those who aren't familiar with bottom bouncers, these strange looking sinkers are simply a piece of wire bent into the shape of an upside down "L". Midway on the long arm a lead weight is molded into place. On the short arm a snap swivel is attached to accept a variety of snelled harnesses. The spinner harness is perhaps the most popular rig used with a bottom bouncer, but these trolling aids can also be used with crankbaits, spoons or simply a straight leader, single hook and leech.

The line tie is located at the elbow between the long and short arms. Some models twist a loop into the wire while others simply bend the wire into an elbow. The models that feature a wire twist will accept a snap or snap swivel making it easier to change from a crankbait to a bottom bouncer rig. Those bouncers with a molded in elbow must be

149

Mike McClelland uses bottom bouncers frequently as a tool to cover water quickly. These unique trolling weights are most often used to catch walleye, but they are just as effective on other species.

150

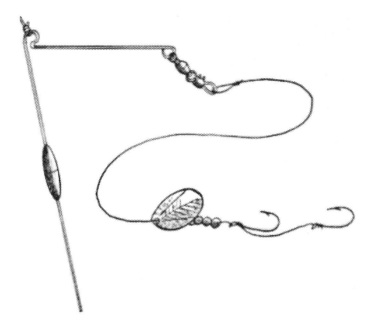

A bottom bouncer is at home when equipped with a snelled spinner rig. For best results the harness should be 48 to 60 inches long.

tied directly to the monofilament.

Designed to present the bait slightly off bottom, these sinkers are also noted for being very snag resistant. When fished properly a bottom bouncer will fish through broken rock and bottom debris that would eat up walking sinkers, bottom walkers and other trolling weights.

A bottom bouncer is also unique because they position the bait in a manner that's easier for fish to eat it. To appreciate what I'm talking about you need to understand how fish feed. All predatory fish feed by opening their mouth and sucking water in through their gills. Like a vaccume cleaner sucking up spilled popcorn, walleye, bass and other fish actually inhale their food along with a mouth full of water. The gill rakers trap the food inside the fish's mouth while letting the water flow through.

When a bottom bouncer is used to troll a bait along structure, the weight itself stops every time it touches bottom, allowing the trailing bait a chance to overrun a little and build slack into the leader. The slack in the leader is what allows the fish to inhale the bait completely.

151

If the fish strikes while the bouncer is moving and the leader is taunt, the bait is simply pulled away from the fish as it attempts to suck in an easy meal. Think about it. In order for the fish to eat a bait pulled on a taunt line it would have to physically overtake the lure and grab it. Most of the time fish simply aren't this aggressive.

Because of the nature of the bottom bouncer and the way these sinkers are fished, they frequently build slack into the leader and allow fish more opportunities to feed naturally. Not surprisingly, bottom bouncers are among the most effective way to fish live bait near bottom.

HOW IT'S DONE

Becoming successful with bottom bouncers starts with some basic knowledge of how to fish these weights. Unlike walking sinkers and other weights that are designed to drag or slide along the bottom, a bottom bouncer should be fished with the wire just off bottom. While trolling the rod tip is dropped back every few feet allowing the bouncer to touch bottom. This touch-and-go style insures that the bait is presented close to the bottom, reduces snags and allows the bottom bouncer to build slack into the leader snell.

A bottom bouncer can be fished effectively using an electric motor a small gasoline kicker motor or drifted. Of these methods trolling using the electric or gasoline motor are the most popular. Drifting can be a good way to cover water and catch fish, but unfortunately drifting depends on the right conditions from Mother Nature. Rarely is the wind blowing just the right direction to properly work a point, sand bar or other piece of bottom structure.

Just about any rod and reel combination can be used for trolling bottom bouncers, but most anglers favor a medium action graphite triggerstick in the six to seven foot range. On this rod a baitcasting reel loaded with eight to 17 pound test works best.

It's also important when fishing bottom bouncers to keep the weight touching bottom at approximately a 45 degree angle to the boat. Sometimes called the rule of 45, if too much line is let out while trolling a bottom bouncer, these weights simply drag along the bottom and snag.

Staying at the 45 degree angle requires the angler to take into consideration two elements including trolling speed and bottom bouncer size or weight. Select your trolling speed then pick a size bottom bouncer that can easily be fished at a 45 degree angle.

If you abide by these two simple rules, it's hard not to catch fish with a bottom bouncer.

WHERE TO USE BOTTOM BOUNCERS

A bottom bouncer is among the most versatile of all trolling rigs. These sinkers can be used to cover large flats, or isolated pieces of bottom structure such as points, sunken islands, rock piles, creek channels and a variety of other situations.

Because bottom bouncers can be fished more quickly than other bottom weights, they are the logical choice for working large pieces of structure such as sprawling flats, mid-lake basins or shorelines. When faced with these conditions, I often combine bottom bouncers with in-line trolling boards to achieve a little extra trolling coverage.

The only board suitable for pulling heavy bottom bouncers is the Off Shore Tackle Side-Planer. Other boards simply aren't designed to handle the drag of heavy weights.

When using Side-Planers, I concentrate on setting two lines out on boards and two lines fished as flat lines. Since the lines must be checked frequently to make sure the bait hasn't been stolen by perch or other small fish, it makes sense to use only one board per side.

Bottom bouncers are set the same way when using boards as when fishing them as flat lines. Set the bottom bouncer using the rule of 45 and attach the board onto the line once the ideal bottom bouncer weight and lead length has been determined.

The action of the board bobbing around in the waves actually works to increase the normal stop-and-go action of the bottom bouncer. When using boards with bottom bouncers it's important to troll only in a following sea. Going against the waves makes it very difficult to maintain a constant speed and presentation.

If the target structure is more isolated, or the depth changes rapidly, boards aren't the answer. In these conditions I prefer to flatline bottom bouncers using an electric motor if the water is shallow or calm and a gasoline kicker in deeper water or when faced with wind and waves.

I define shallow water as anything under 10 feet. In these conditions I favor the electric motor unless the wind is really blowing.

When working precise pieces of structure it's often best to pick a depth level and stay with it. Work out all the structure at a particular depth, then switch to the next deepest contour.

There is however an exception worth noting. One of the ways I frequently target big fish is by working steep breaks. Large walleye, bass and pike often call these edges home. Many times these fish simply cruise the edge at different depth levels looking for something foolish enough to stray within striking distance.

When targeting these edges with bottom bouncers I'm actually using the bottom bouncer to fish both the vertical and horizontal plane. Instead of using a blade harness I'll use a five foot leader with a shallow diving crankbait such as a Rebel Minnow or Smithwick Rattlin' Rogue. It's best to start on top of the structure and using an electric motor slide the nose of the boat out off the edge of the break. Let the bottom bouncer sink into the water thumbing it down to prevent a backlash. Once the bait hits bottom, swing the boat around and work your way back up the edge again.

In most instances if a big fish is present it will strike the first time the bait comes by. This unusual technique has produced many of the biggest fish I've taken on bottom bouncers.

OTHER GUIDELINES

Some of the other guidelines worth noting are water color. Bottom bouncers are often most effective in water that's dirty or off color. In gin clear water the weight itself may spook some fish before the bait even gets to them.

When fishing blades harnesses, I let the water clarity be my guide to blade size. The clearer the water the smaller the blade I select. In dirty water you can't fish too big a blade.

Harness length is also an important consideration. For trolling blade harnesses the ideal length for the harness is 48-60 inches. If the harness is longer it will drag on the bottom and become snagged. If the harness is shorter, the bait is presented too close to the bottom bouncer weight.

154

When I'm pulling blades the harnesses I use are tied using 12-17 pound test monofilament. If I'm using a snell and single hook the ideal leader length is the same as with blades, but I'd opt for six or eight pound test monofilament to give the bait a little more freedom to swim.

The bait you use is also something to ponder. When fishing blade harnesses nightcrawlers are the number one bait. For best results these crawlers should be conditioned into a fat and beefy mouthful. A good way to condition nightcrawlers is to place a few in a wet towel filled with crushed ice. As the ice melts the crawlers absorb the water and swell up like little snakes.

Minnows can also be used on blade harnesses, but they must be pulled slowly to avoid line twist. When using minnows it's also critical to hook the bait lightly through both lips so the bait pulls straight in the water.

When fishing a snell and single hook, I'm almost always using a leech for bait. Nothing beats the swimming action of a leech worked behind a bottom bouncer. The key when fishing leeches is to troll very slowly. If you troll leeches too fast, the bait simply rolls up into a ball on the hook.

Another bottom bouncer tip worth mentioning involves open water trolling. Often walleye found in open water suspend at different depth levels. A bottom bouncer combined with in-line boards is a great tool for covering these different depth ranges.

A few years ago I won the Lake Erie PWT tournament held at Put-in-Bay Ohio by fishing bottom bouncers in open water. I was fishing mud flats in 40 feet of water with walleye suspended all over the place.

I set out a one ounce bottom bouncer and spinner combination 30 feet and cliped on an in-line board. One of these rigs was fished off each side of the boat. Then I fished two three way rigs with three ounce weights straight behind the boat.

The waves were averaging five to six foot at this particular tournament. I trolled with the waves and used my boat to speed up and slow down the presentation. Each time I throttled up my kicker motor the outside bottom bouncer lines were forced to rise in the water column, then when I slowed down those lines began to sink through the schools of suspended fish.

155

Using four lines, two set to fish the suspended fish and two set to hug the bottom, I was able to take walleye almost at will. Most of the fish came on the board lines, but the biggest fish came from the bottom.

CLOSING THOUGHTS

In closing it's important to remember that the deeper you fish a bottom bouncer the slower you'll be forced to troll. At some point you'll be going so slow that a blade simply won't rotate properly. In deep water a snell with a single hook or a crankbait are among the best options. In shallow water situations it's tough to beat a blade harness.

Bottom bouncers are my number one tool for locating walleye on unfamiliar water, and they are also one of my most productive methods for catching fish. Equally effective on bass, pike and other species, if you don't own a boat full of bottom bouncers, you need to get the lead out and watch how something as simple as a piece of wire and lead can work magic on bottom orientated fish.

In the next chapter we'll take a look at trolling under the light of a Coleman lantern. Trolling after dark is one of the least practiced, yet most effective ways to catch trophy class fish.

Mike McClelland is a walleye tournament pro and a member of the Fishing Hall Of Fame.

Captain John Hook is a night trolling specialist that uses his techniques to catch trophy walleye, bass, salmon and other species.

157

Chapter 17

Trolling After Dark
By
John Hook

A lot of anglers are trolling in the dark, and a few are actually fishing after the sun goes down!

In all seriousness, some anglers become so addicted to night trolling that their eyes get small as crawler harness beads and they develop a keen sense of echo location. Well maybe the part about the small eyes and echo location is a stretch, but it's true that a dedicated group of anglers are discovering how exciting and productive trolling after dark can be.

When the subject of night fishing comes up, talk normally focuses on walleye. It's well known that this species is cleverly adapted to feeding after dark. What many anglers don't realize is that lots of other species are equally suited to feeding after dark. Just a few of the fish you're likely to catch in the dark include, largemouth and smallmouth bass, steelhead, musky, channel catfish, trout and even salmon.

When you troll after dark, you never know what will bite your lures. In fact, many species do the majority of their foraging from sunset to sunrise. This is especially true of trophy sized specimens. Not unlike a trophy whitetail buck bent on keeping his antlers, oversized walleye, bass and other fish learn that the dark periods of the clock are among the most safe and productive times to feed.

Some anglers may argue that certain species of fish have simply evolved as nocturnal animals. It's true that walleye for example are well adapted to feeding after dark. Their large eyes pick up every available ray of light, not unlike the large objective lens on a pair of binoculars or a rifle scope. This feature allows them to see better in the dark than other

158

species, but it's not so much vision, but the lateral line sense that allows walleye and other fish to feed effectively in low light conditions.

The lateral line sense works like radar to help detect objects in the water, determine their size, the direction and speed they are traveling and even confirm the exact species based on a sound signature that's unique to each different kind of fish. All this data is processed by the lateral line and sent to the brain in a matter of a millisecond.

The lateral line is an organ, not an instinctive sense. Because the lateral line is an internal organ it stands to reason that it becomes more acute as the fish matures. Some anglers are convinced that walleye and other species of fish combine their finely tuned lateral line sense with learned responses. Collectively, the fish uses these skills and knowledge to form a feeding strategy that focuses their hunting efforts at a time when prey are at a disadvantage and the threat of predators is reduced.

This combination of fact and theory suggests that the best time to catch a trophy walleye or other species is after sunset. Continuing to use walleye as an example, consider the large number of trophy walleye that have been caught after dark, compared to the rather limited fishing effort focused at night. The data screams one simple conclusion; fish after dark.

If it were legal to hunt deer after dark, there would be no trophy bucks left. Yet, there's no threat that night fishermen will overharvest the walleye population any time soon. A small minority of anglers are willing to fish in the dark, despite the obvious rewards.

TRADITIONAL TACTICS

Trolling after dark has traditionally been targeted primarily at walleye and bass. This night trolling game has simple rules. For the most part the lures incorporated are crankbaits and the primary technique used is best described as a modified form of flatline trolling.

Instead of simply putting the rods in holders and power trolling, the most successful anglers hold their rods, adding a pumping action that helps to trigger following or nearby fish. Also, in an effort to remain as quiet as possible, powerful electric motors are used in place of gasoline outboards to silently slip along at speeds from 1 to 1.5 mph.

The spots targeted with this simple angling technique are classics. Rip rap banks, sea walls, weed lines, channel edges, sunken islands and

159

piles of submerged wood or debris are a few of the logical targets.

Floating/diving style crankbaits are selected because the diving depth of these baits can be determined and duplicated. Sinking lures tend to be speed dependant, making them very difficult to control when fishing close to potential snags such as broken rock, brush or weeds.

The lead lengths and pound test line used are monitored closely so as to determine the exact lure diving depth. The whole secret to this style of trolling is to fish as close as possible to bottom structure or cover without getting snagged up.

Several times in this book we've referred to the publication Precision Trolling. Once again this unique product is the guide that most night trollers use to determine the diving depth of over 120 different crankbaits. Using the dive curves contained within this book, anglers can be certain of lure diving depth within six inches plus or minus!

Usually, but not always, the best lures are large stickbaits. Large lures create more disturbance in the water, making it easier for fish to locate the bait. Also, the larger size of the lure increases the chances that a striking fish will actually make contact with the bait and get hooked.

Jointed lures are also popular choices because they have maximum action at the slowest possible speeds. Baits such as the Storm Jointed ThunderStick, Rebel Jointed Fastrac, Rapala Jointed Minnow and Sparkletail are classic night fishing lures.

THE BOARD TROLLING TWIST

The growing popularity of in-line boards such as the Off Shore Tackle Side-Planer has lead a few adventuresome anglers to experiment with board fishing after dark. This unorthodox method of fishing is deadly, yet surprisingly few anglers have tried it.

To fish an in-line board effectively you must be able to see the board. When a fish is hooked the board pulls backwards in the water from the weight of the struggling fish. Essentially the board becomes a strike detector, but not if you can't see the board in the dark.

Anglers are using a number of ingenious methods that make in-line boards an effective way to fish after dark. The three inch cylume sticks provide just enough light to see the boards even on the darkest nights.

In-line planer boards are handy tools for trolling at night. Note that a cylume stick has been attached to the flag to make the board easy to spot on the water.

These chemical activated light sources are inexpensive, readily available, they come in different colors and they last long enough to enjoy a full night of trolling. The time to stock up on cylume sticks is after Holloween when retailers clearance out stock not sold to trick-or-treaters.

Bend the cylume stick to activate the light, shake it a few times to insure it glows brightly. Next, take a couple wire wraps to attach it to the flag of the Side-Planer. The green lights seem to show up best, but some anglers prefer to run one color on the port side and another color on the starboard. This color coding system helps other anglers on the water tell which direction you're trolling.

Another trick that helps to detect strikes involves the bait clickers located on most levelwind style reels. Once the leads are set, boards attached and positioned out to the side, place the rod in a rod holder and back off on the drag until line slipping off the spool activates the bait clicker. Tighten the drag just enough to prevent line from clicking out and wait. When a fish strikes the clicker with immediately identify the rod that has hooked a fish.

In-line boards can be fished effectively using small gasoline kickers or powerful electric motors. This unique trolling technique can be used almost anywhere and for lots of different species. Shallow diving cranks pulled over the tops of weed flats is a deadly way to fool largemouth bass. You can even use top water baits such as the Jitterbug, Crazy Crawler or Devil's Horse behind boards. Fish with a stop and go trolling pattern that adds action to the lures and watch it drive bass crazy.

Smallmouth that live on rock and gravel flats are also likely victims of night fishing. Use cranks that dive to within a foot or two of bottom and hold on. Smallies slam lures fished at night like its their last meal.

Walleye are prime targets for in-line boards when these fish suspend to feed on shad, alewives or smelt. Usually the best night fishing for walleye takes place in early spring and again in the fall, but any time of year can produce explosive results.

Steelhead and salmon are also eager to feed after dark. Trolling spoons, stickbaits and small diving cranks around Great Lakes pier heads is a fast way to boat a limit of these chrome rockets.

Inland lakes with populations of lake, brook, brown or rainbow trout are also targets for night trolling and in-line boards. Trout will hit a wide variety of trolling spoons, small crankbaits and spinners pulled behind in-line boards. An excellent trout fishing trick is to pull blade harnesses baited with fat nightcrawlers or live minnows behind boards.

TIPS FOR SMOOTH TROLLING

Trolling after dark can be amazingly effective, but this style of fishing isn't without its share of frustrations. Safety is a major concern when fishing after dark. Be absolutely sure your boat is equipped with dependable bow and stern running lights and use them at all times. Also it's important to make sure your cranking and accessory batteries are in good shape and fully charged.

When you leave home for a night of trolling, be sure to tell someone exactly where you'll be fishing and when you expect to return. Don't vary from this game plan unless you inform someone of your change in plans.

You'll also need some type of light on board when it's time to tie on lures, unhook fish or just to find a sandwich in the dark. A flashlight is a good start, but the light generated from a hand-held flash light is tough to work by. A better solution is a battery powered lantern. Many of these lights are adjustable so the angler can conserve battery juice as needed.

Some anglers mount halogen style flood lights at the back of their boat. The lights are wired directly to the battery and a convenient switch positioned where it can be easily found in the dark. When a fish is hooked the flood lights are turned on to make it easy to spot and net struggling fish. Once the fish is untangled from the net and released or placed in the livewell, the bright lights are turned off again.

A final concern regarding night trolling is to always keep a neat and clean boat. In the dark fishing lines and lures have a nasty habit of catching on things. When you change lures, put the used bait back into the tackle box, so it doesn't end up stuck into something it shouldn't be.

Designate a spot for important items like your net, line clippers or pliers and always put them back after using them. Trolling in the dark requires organization if everything is to run smoothly.

This chapter just touches on the tip of the iceberg when it comes to night trolling. The first step is to accept the idea of fishing when others

When the sun goes down fishing for many species picks up. Walleye, bass, salmon, steelhead, musky and other species all bite readily at night.

are sleeping and then get out and identify opportunities close to home. A wide variety of species can be targeted after dark, and who knows your catch may just include something worth bragging about.

John Hook is a tournament pro and a night fishing specialist.

Trolling is a dirty word in some bass fishing circles. Ironically, trolling is one of the best ways to find and catch bass. With the catch and release attitude anglers share today, does it matter how you catch them?

166

Chapter 18

Bass Trolling Tactics
By
Mark Romanack

Bass and trolling are two words you seldom see in the same sentence. An unwritten taboo exists when it comes to trolling for bass. This prejudice dates back to the early days of bass fishing when trolling in it's many forms was banned from competitive fishing.

Those who emulate professional bass fishermen have followed suit by treating trolling like it was incurable disease. Despite the fact that there's no ethical, moral or biological reason why bass anglers can't troll, you rarely see anyone serious enough to put fishing patches on his jacket practicing the act of pulling baits.

Being dedicated to bass angling is one thing, but refusing to troll simply because tournament pros aren't allowed to in competition rates as one of the great all time acts of stubbornness. It's crazy for anglers to limit the legitimate fishing methods available to them. Limiting the way a person fishes is the same as limiting how many fish they can catch.

Think about it; putting restrictions on angling techniques and the fun of catching fish isn't what this sport is all about. Tradition and peer pressure cause folks to do a lot of things for the wrong reasons. Don't let these forces keep you from trolling and catching more bass.

BREAKING THE ICE

Once you've digested the idea of trolling for bass, the angling opportunities available will send your mind whirling. Bass are an ideal target for trolling because these fish are aggressive predators that are constantly on the move in search of forage. Both largemouth and smallmouth bass often travel in packs or loose schools that once located can provide exciting action. Trolling for bass also makes sense because like walleye

167

and other species, the best concentrations of fish tend to be found in a relatively limited portion of the available habitat.

The very reason that trolling is so popular among walleye and salmon fishermen has been conveniently ignored by the average bass angler. Trolling covers water quickly and is the best way to located fish that may be scattered over hundreds or even thousands of acres of water.

Even if trolling is used only to locate fish, this powerful fish finding technique is invaluable to anyone wanting to catch more bass. Use trolling tactics to locate fish then switch over to traditional methods if you like, but don't overlook the value of trolling.

I remember a walleye tournament I fished way up at Rainy Lake along the Minnesota and Ontario borders. It was late summer and most of the walleye were holding on classic deep water structure. Sunken islands and rock piles were lousy with walleye. For every walleye I caught trolling bottom bouncers, two smallmouth bass stood in line to eat my wiggling leeches. I didn't mind catching the smallmouth, even though they made it hard to catch the less aggressive walleye.

After the tournament was over, I went out fishing just for fun and pounded on some of the finest smallmouth bass I've ever seen. If it hadn't been for trolling, I might never have found those eager smallmouth.

EQUIPMENT NEEDS

Serious bass fishermen already own most of the equipment they need to enjoy trolling. Just about any boat with a few rod holders and a powerful electric motor or a small gasoline outboard can be used to troll up bass. Despite rumors to the contrary, even fancy bass boats can be used!

Straight handle triggersticks make excellent trolling rods. Medium or medium/light action rods ranging from six to seven feet long are ideal. These rods should be equipped with baitcasting reels loaded with premium 10 to 17 pound test monofilament. Lighter line is used when trolling in open areas such as flats where snags aren't a concern. When trolling among or near cover, using heavier line is a good option.

When trolling for bass, crankbaits are the primary lures used. Most bass anglers already have an excellent selection of these baits. Many of the models that are favorites among casters are also ideal for trolling.

168

The best models for trolling are ones that float at rest and dive when pulled. Sinking baits like the famous Rat-L-Trap are excellent casting lures, but it's difficult to control their running depth when trolling. All sinking lures are speed dependant or in other words trolling speed dictates their running depth.

The running depth of floating/diving crankbaits can easily be controlled by manipulating lead length. The longer the lead length used the deeper these lures dive. Of course other factors such as the size of the lure's diving lip, buoyancy and the diameter of the fishing line used also influence crankbait diving depth.

The book Precision Trolling which has been referred to several times in this publication provides an invaluable guide to crankbait diving depth. The trollers bible, this unique publication offers a wealth of fishing data, tips and related information that make the trolling game easier to master.

In-line boards are an important trolling item that the average bass fishermen probably doesn't own. The Off Shore Tackle Side-Planer runs about $20.00 and has become the board of choice across the nation. Just about everything that swims has fallen prey to these little planer boards.

Side-Planer boards come in left and right versions. One set of boards is a good starting point, but most anglers end up purchasing two sets once they see how productive in-line board trolling can be.

Boards enable anglers to spread out their trolling lines to cover more water and to fish additional lines. In-line boards are the logical choice for bass fishing because they are inexpensive, can be stored in any tackle box or boat and are easy to use with traditional bass fishing tackle.

Another piece of trolling equipment that bass anglers aren't likely to own are bottom bouncer sinkers. Bottom bouncers are simply a piece of wire bent into the shape of an upside down "L". On the long arm a weight is molded midway on the wire shaft. The short arm features a snap swivel that accepts an elongated version of the garden variety nightcrawler harness. The fishing line is tied to the bottom bouncer where the two arms meet and the whole rig is slow trolled (dragged) along with the long arm walking over bottom debris.

A popular rig for trolling walleye on structure, bottom bouncers can be dragged over gravel flats, rocks, downed timber and lots of other fish

169

holding structure with minimal hang-ups. When using bottom bouncer sinkers to troll for bass, several terminal tackle options are available. The most common choice is a 48 to 60 inch long snelled crawler harness, baited with a live crawler or one of the scent impregnated plastic worms.

The combination of the flashing and gurgling blade and live bait is more than any self respecting bass can take. When fishing this rig where bluegill or other panfish are abundant, scented plastic worms are more durable and stay on the hook better.

Another option for the bottom bouncer is simply a plain 60 inch snell equipped with a single hook and a live leech, minnow or nightcrawler. This option works best when trolled very slowly and is deadly on bass that take up residence in deep water around sunken islands or channel edges.

A third option substitutes the single hook and live bait for a shallow diving crankbait. With the help of bottom bouncers, small or shallow diving crankbaits fished on a 48 to 60 inch leader can be easily fished in water up to 40 feet deep.

METHODS TO THE MADNESS

Adding methods to the madness of trolling for bass is the next step. There are countless ways to troll for bass, but a few methods are so universal that they demand mention.

Trolling crankbaits with the use of in-line boards is one of those methods. Any time that bass are spread out on flats, suspended in open water, concentrated on rock or gravel bottom structure or feeding in sparse weed cover, a trolled crankbait is the logical way to catch them.

Crankbaits can be trolled directly behind the boat by simply trolling in a series of "S" turns that sweep the baits out away from noise of the outboard or the boat moving through the water. An even more effective way to troll is by incorporating in-line boards like the Side-Planer to achieve better trolling coverage.

The Side-Planer is easy to fish. Begin by setting a favorite crankbait the desired distance behind the boat. Attach the Side-Planer onto the line by opening the pinch pad release at the front of the board and placing the

Bass are often caught by accident while trolling for other species. Marilyn DeShano caught this one while hunting for walleye on a southern impoundment.

line midway between the rubber pads. Repeat this process with the release at the back of the board and place it in the water. As the boat trolls forward slowly let line off from the reel allowing the board to track out to the side.

Those who troll boards religiously usually fish two or three boards per side. Beginners to board trolling can get the feel of this trolling style by placing one board out each side and fishing a flat line or two directly out the back of the boat.

When a fish strikes the lures trolled behind the Side-Planer you'll know it immediately. The acrobatic fish they are, bass are usually tailwalking behind the board seconds after being hooked. If the fish decides not to jump, the weight of the struggling fish pulls the board sharply backwards in the water.

Without stopping the boat, get the rod in hand and slowly reel in the board and fish together. Once the board is close enough to reach, simply pinch open the line releases and remove the board from the line. It takes longer to describe how to remove an in-line board than it takes to do it.

When two boards are fished per side and a fish is hooked on the outside board, the angler first reels in the inside line and places it out of the way on the opposite side of the boat. Once the line is cleared, the fish can be fought without fear of tangling lines.

Once the board is removed, slow down or stop the boat and fight the fish to net. This basic method of trolling crankbaits can be applied to a wide variety of bass fishing situations. Shallow diving stickbaits can be pulled over the tops of emerging weeds, crawfish imitating lures can be trolled along bottom structure or shad shaped lures can be used to fool suspended bass that often feed on schools of gizzard and threadfin shad. These are just a few of the trolling situations anglers encounter.

Trolling bottom bouncers is another unorthodox method of fishing bass that can pay big dividends when these fish are found on isolated bottom real estate or wide open flats.

The bottom bouncer sinkers described earlier in this chapter are widely available across the northern half of this land where they are used mostly for walleye fishing. In the south, southeast and southwest anglers are probably going to be forced to mail order a supply from places such as

Diving crankbaits like this Hot 'N Tot are excellent choices when trolling for bass. This dandy smallmouth was taken off a gravel shoal that held lots of fish.

Cabela's 812 13th Avenue, Sidney, NE 69160 or the Walleye Specialties Catalog, C/O Bass Pro Shops, 1935 S. Campbell, Springfield, MO 65898.

The bottom bouncer brings several key elements to the trolling scene. Perhaps the most important aspect of trolling with bottom bouncers is the action these wire sinkers impart to lures and baits.

When a bottom bouncer is fished properly it walks along bottom in a rocking motion that pulls the bait forward on a taunt line, then hesitates for a second and allows the bait to slow down, stop or in some cases flutter down for a split second. This stop and go motion drives bass and other fish crazy and it also builds a little slack in the leader making it easier for the attacking fish to get the bait past its lips.

Another virtue of bottom bouncers is these trolling weights are very snag resistant and can be fished in areas that would eat up slip sinkers, walking sinkers and split shots. Also, the shape of these wire trolling aids helps to position the trailing lures just a few inches off bottom.

When fishing bottom bouncers there are some hard and fast rules that must be followed. To keep the sinker walking over bottom, the bottom bouncer must be fished at approximately a 45 degree angle from the boat to the bottom. If too much line is let out the weight simply lays on its side and gets dragged along the bottom. When this happens, the features that make trolling bottom bouncers so effective are lost.

In order to maintain this delicate balance, the angler must choose a bottom bouncer size based on water depth and trolling speed. Available in sizes from 1/4 ounce to four ounces, the most common sizes are 1/2, 1, 1.5 and 2 ounces.

It's better to use a bottom bouncer that's a little too heavy than one that's too light. It's also best to set the bouncer to run a little off the bottom, rather than allowing the weight to maintain constant contact with bottom. If the bottom bouncer lightly ticks along bottom, touching down every few feet that's perfect.

At the business end of a bottom bouncer it's tough to beat a 48 to 60 inch long nightcrawler harness or what walleye fishermen refer to as a spinner rig. A size 1, 2 or 3 Colorado or Indiana style blade is one of the best possible attractors and when combined with a live nightcrawler the party is all but over for nearby bass.

174

The bottom bouncer and spinner combination functions best as a fish finding tool since it can be pulled at a fairly brisk speed. Once fish are located more traditional tackle and methods can be used to catch fish or a different twist tried with the bottom bouncer.

Once fish are located a different bottom bouncer rigging option makes sense. Switching to a plain 60 inch snell with a single hook baited with a leech, minnow or nightcrawler enables the angler to slow down and work key structure more throughly.

Using an electric or gasoline motor to barely move the boat along, the bottom bouncer is used to simply keep track of the bottom, while the trailing live bait swims naturally.

This simple technique is absolutely dynamite when smallmouth bass crowd into deep water structure such as sunken islands, creek channels, rock piles or along submerged brush piles.

During the spring and summer, leeches, nightcrawlers, small minnows or live crawfish are the best live bait choices. In the fall, bass prefer a bigger mouthful. Using this technique with a four to six inch sucker, chub or dace minnow often produces monster bass.

Unfortunately, for the masses who enjoy bass fishing there's a stigma associated with trolling for these species. The way I look at it, trolling is a great way to find and catch fish; and what Roland Martin, Larry Nixon and David Fritts don't know won't hurt them!

In chapter 19 the focus turns to electric motor trolling. The stealth of an electric motor is important to many trolling applications.

Two time Angler-of-the-Year Kevin VanDam took this nice bass near his Michigan home with the help of an electric trolling motor.

Chapter 19
Electric Motor Trolling
By
Bruce DeShano

The electric trolling motor is the best thing to impact on sport fishing since the invention of sonar. So common has this fishing aid become that we take them for granted. Most serious fishermen would be lost without the help of an electric motor to position the boat and move it along silently.

To say that electric motors have been refined in recent years is a bit of an understatement. The earliest models of electric motors were designed to fit over the transom of the boat and operated off a 12 volt battery. Intended for backtrolling, it quickly became obvious that controlling a boat from the back with an electric motor is awkward in the best of conditions and downright frustrating when the wind picks up. The demand for bow mounted electric motors was soon realized and soon after and the race to improve these units picked up momentum.

One of the first improvements centered on the power or pound thrust generated. Motors that operated using 12 volts simply couldn't muster enough thrust to fish hard all day in windy conditions. Doubling the voltage output to 24 volts made it possible to squeeze twice as much power and service from an electric motor. Eventually even 24 volt systems weren't deemed adequate. Some of the newer motors today feature 36 volts of power that generate upwards of 70 foot pounds of on-demand thrust. The MotorGuide Beast is one of the more popular 36 volt systems.

This powerful 36 volt systems is favored by serious bass and walleye tournament pros who are forced to fish long hours in difficult conditions. The average consumer will find that 24 volt systems are more than

177

adequate in most fishing situations.

Early bow mounted units were hand operated. Hand operated bow mount motors are still available today from the leading manufacturers, but foot controlled units have become the more popular choice. Most of these motors use a foot operated cable system to move the power head.

Some time later, radio controlled products hit the market that use a radio frequency to control the motor's speed and direction. Radio frequency motors can be operated from any position in the boat, allowing the angler freedom to fish where comfortable. The MotorGuide Lazer and Lazer II are two examples of radio controlled electric motors.

As high tech as radio frequency electric motors are, even more sophisticated units are available. The Pinpoint Electric Motor goes a step further and actually uses a computer that senses bottom contours and allows the motor to follow a pre-determined contour or depth.

The ultimate means for trolling along meandering breaks or edge, these units operate by sound waves transmitted through a transducer much like a sonar transducer. The transducer signals indicates changes in depth and an on-board computer senses these changes. The motor head is moved accordingly and the boat stays on course.

Other electric motors act as auto-pilots. Both MotorGuide and Minn Kota produce auto-pilot style electric motors. These units require the user to program a desired direction. Once the direction is set the motor will follow this course, making adjustments for drift created by wind, waves or current.

The advancements in electric motors we are currently enjoying may be just the tip of the carrot. There are even electric motor brackets that raise and lower the motor for you. Imagine that. No one knows for sure how technology will make our electric motor trolling easier, more productive and functional.

WHY ELECTRIC MOTORS?

With so many quality gasoline motors on the market, the question remains why do so many anglers turn to electric motors for boat control? The answer to this question can be summed up in one word "stealth". The ability to control the boat while making the least amount of noise and disturbance is critical in many fishing situations.

Bow mounted electric trolling motors are an invaluable fishing tool when fishing clear or shallow water. Smallmouth like this are just one of the many fish that can be taken with the help of electric motors.

Even the super quiet four stroke outboards currently available can't come close to the quiet power electric motors provide. Electric motors are also more maneuverable. Because the head can be turned in a full 360 radius, electric motors have a huge advantage over gasoline motors when it comes to boat control chores.

Granted, electric motors aren't suitable for all trolling needs, especially open water or speed trolling applications. These situations clearly call for a gasoline kicker, but for a wealth of fishing presentations the quiet trolling power of an electric motor is the answer.

Electric motors fill such an important boat control niche, that few boats these days are sold without one. The biggest problem that occurs with electric motors isn't the brand or style of motor chosen, but rather the power the unit generates. Anglers have a tendency to under power their boats in an effort to save a little cash. Boat dealers routinely under power their boats to keep the total boat/motor/trailer package price less shocking.

It's understandable why anglers and marine dealers sometimes cut corners when it comes to electric motors. The better models on the market may cost upwards of $500.00 and many run two or three times this amount. Still, cost factors aside nothing controls a boat like a good electric motor.

When selecting an electric motor it's better to purchase a unit that's a little more powerful than necessary, than to always find yourself short on power. The largest 12 volt units generated 30-40 foot pounds of trust or enough to control an aluminum boat up to 16 feet long. For larger aluminum boats or heavier fiberglass hulls the extra power of a 24 volt system is recommended. Many of these motors produce over 60 foot pounds of thrust, more than enough to control even heavy fiberglass boats for a full day of fishing.

The next mistake anglers make is purchasing a shaft length that's too short for the boat it's mounted on. If the motor barely reaches the water, the prop will blow out every time the boat bobs up and down in waves and maintaining good control will be impossible.

Bow mounted electric motors come with various length shafts ranging from 40-60 inches. Longer 50, 54 or 60 inch shafts are required to reach the water with deep "V" style boats. Low sitting bass boats and many small aluminum boats can get by nicely with a 40 inch shaft.

Selecting quality deep cycle batteries and maintaining them is the next step to trouble free electric motor use. Purchase the largest amp rating batteries you can find. High amp batteries such as those that deliver upwards of 100 amps provide longer service at high output.

The best way to maintain these batteries is with a waterproof style electronic charging unit that mounts in the boat. While these solid state chargers cost considerably more than portable units, they can charge two or three batteries at the same time. Each battery is charged to capacity then the charger automatically shuts off. A series of LED lights shows the stages of the charging process.

A quality electric motor, good batteries and a dependable charging system add up to trouble-free service. Most problems that occur with electric motors can be traced to battery or charging problems.

GETTING STARTED

Trolling with an electric motor is as easy as pointing in the direction you want to go. Cable driven foot control models require a little practice to master basic maneuvers. After a short time the operator gets a sense for the direction the motor is pointed by how his or her foot is positioned on the foot cable control. Most anglers are comfortable with cable driven units after playing with them for an hour or two.

The more sophisticated directional controlled, radio controlled and auto-pilot motors are just as easy to master. Plan on spending a little time getting used to these products before going on a serious fishing trip.

Most electric motors have a continuous-on function that bypasses the rocker switch on the foot control. Use this function when trolling along a break, over sprawling flats or other areas where the boat must be moved a considerable distance. Use the rocker style power switch for smaller boat control jobs.

WHEN TO USE ELECTRIC MOTORS

Part of getting the most from an electric trolling motor is knowing when to use these products and when a small gasoline motor is the better option. Electric motors shine best in clear and/or shallow water fishing

181

This boat is equipped with both a transom and bow mounted electric motor. Transom mounted units are handy for backtrolling chores, but for other boat control methods a bow mounted unit is more practical.

conditions. In clear water fish are more spooky and difficult to approach with outboard motors. The quiet power an electric motor provides is a clear advantage when fishing in clear water.

A similar conclusion can be made when fishing in shallow water. Even if the water is turbid or off color, it's tough to approach fish close enough to catch them in water less than 10 feet deep. The shallower the water to be fished, the more beneficial electric trolling motors become.

Calm conditions are a third situation when an electric trolling motor can be an advantage. When the water's surface is calm fish are espe-

182

cially difficult to approach. The reason for this fact is simple. Fish sense other objects moving in the water by using their lateral line. An organ located just under the surface of the skin, this highly refined sense acts like radar helping fish detect both vibrations and water displacement caused when objects move through the water.

How acute is the lateral line sense? A walleye or bass can easily detect a minnow swimming many yards away. Not only does the fish know the minnow is there, it can also determine its size, the direction it's traveling and speed.

The lateral line is the primary reason predatory fish such as walleye, bass, stripers and others are able to feed effectively even in turbid water. As refined as the lateral line is, when wave action moves the water this sensory system is dulled.

Have you ever heard that the best time to fish walleye is during a breeze that puts a chop on the water? The reason fish like walleye bite better in these conditions is because anglers are able to approach them more closely without being detected.

In calm water conditions the vibrations of a gasoline motor and the water displacement created by the boat insures that fish in the area will sense the boat coming and move away long before it arrives. An electric motor is able to move the boat with less sound and vibration and is therefore a better choice when faced with calm waters.

Night fishing is another period when electric motors out perform gasoline trolling motors. For the same reasons described when fishing in calm water, night trolling screams for the features of an electric motor.

Also, under the cover of darkness fish feel a sense of security that sometimes lures them out away from cover to hunt in open water. When fish hunt in open water they are much more vulnerable to predators. Not surprisenly, these fish are constantly alert to approaching danger and difficult to approach. On the flip side, when fish move out away from cover they are also more susceptible to angling pressure. Fishing after dark is such an important aspect of trolling that the next chapter has been dedicated to this unique and interesting form of fishing.

Electric trolling motors are a piece of the trolling puzzle, just like lures, rods, reels, electronics, boats and many other pieces of fishing

183

equipment. Often taken for granted, the electric motor enables us to catch fish in challenging situations that would be nearly impossible to overcome using a gasoline motor.

Chapter 20
Open Water Trolling Tactics For Musky & Pike

By
Don Miller

The sport we affectionately call fishing is made up from as much mythology as fact. This is especially true when talk turns to the muskellunge. The largest member of the Esox or pike family, anglers who fish for musky have been known to exaggerate a little. Surprisingly, the exaggerations aren't centered so much on the size of the fish. Musky are commonly taken in the 30 pound class and occasionally a fish upwards of 50 pounds is landed! It's a fact that musky grow big wherever you find them, but despite their often huge size these fish aren't the mystical and elusive predator of the deep that anglers make them out to be.

Musky aren't nearly as difficult to catch as you might imagine and they certainly don't have the brain power to think their way out of being captured by sportfishing pressure. The number of musky taken in most waters is low simply because the population of fish per acre of water is equally low. Natural lakes, backwaters and sluggish streams can only support a limited number of these primary predators, just like the grasslands of Africa can only support so many lions.

When musky are exposed to larger environments with ample food, cover and spawning habitat, their numbers increase dramatically. Simply put, these large waters support more and larger fish.

Lake St. Clair is a prime example of a world class musky fishery. I've fished this sprawling lake since the early 70's and have run a full time charter business for 12 years. During this period I'm comfortable in saying my customers have caught over 2500 adult musky. I'm also proud to report that over 90% of these fish have been photographed, weighed and measured for a graphite replica mount then released to fight again.

185

Captain Don Miller produces over 300 musky per year for his customers. His trolling tactics were developed from musky fishing legend Homer LeBlanc.

186

In recent years I've averaged over 300 adult fish per year. A good day of fishing on Lake St. Clair can yield as many as eight legal musky! Compared to the world famous musky waters of Northern Wisconsin, well lets just say that Lake St. Clair is in a class all itself.

Anglers who work the traditional musky waters of Wisconsin, Minnesota and southern Ontario often fish for days without even getting a follow. With fishing conditions like these, it's easy to see where the slogan of musky fishing, ie: the fish of a thousand casts, gets its roots.

For the record, virtually every fish I've landed on Lake St. Clair has been taken using trolling tactics developed by my mentor and friend the late Homer LeBlanc. Homer helped me understand the musky as a game fish and taught me how to take advantage of it's opportunistic feeding habits.

Understanding what makes a musky tick is the key to catching these awesome trophies. An adult musky is a fish with an attitude. An attitude that develops simply from being on the top of the food chain. Imagine how you might act if you were the largest fish in your environment and capable of eating almost anything that swims. Musky have no natural predators once they reach adult size. Sport fishing pressure is the only threat to musky survival.

I believe that musky have an attitude similar to that of a lion. These efficient predators are opportunistic eating what they can get and when they can get it. Usually this translates into forage that strays too close to their powerful jaws and sharp teeth. The list of foods musky eat is a long one, starting with injured, sick or dying baitfish, followed closely by other species of fish such as suckers, drum, yellow perch, bass, walleye, northern pike and even young musky. For additional protein these fish have also been known to take ducklings, young muskrats, frogs, snakes and just about anything else that ends up in the water.

I've taken some strange things out of the stomachs of musky over the years including red and white bobbers, various pieces of trash and even an adult walleye that must have weighed five or six pounds!

The startling thing about trophy musky is it's obvious they are capable of eating prey much larger than the largest fishing lures designed to catch these giants. Can you imagine trolling with a 20 inch long Believer or

187

casting a two pound Dardevle. Sound crazy? Sure, but the fact remains that musky survive in part by feeding on large forage that allows them to feed less often.

The fact that musky are somewhat selective in their feeding habits is one of the major reasons I'm convinced that trolling is the most efficient means of catching these fish. Trolling, especially the speed trolling tactics developed by Homer LeBlanc, generate a reactionary type strike from musky as aposed to casting or slow trolling which allows the fish the opportunity to follow and scrutinize the baits.

I'm not saying that musky swim up and look at slow moving baits, then make a conscious decision that the bait is a fake. More likely, slow moving baits trigger a following response because the fish knows it can catch this meal any time it chooses.

Faster moving baits don't allow musky the luxury of following the bait like a wolf follows an injured deer waiting for the right moment to pounce. When a fast moving bait passes by a musky his instinctive reactions take over and the rest of the story is history.

Trolling is the only practical way to move baits at the speeds it takes to trigger a reactionary strike from large predators like musky. Sure you can cast lures and reel them in quickly to achieve the same effect, but can you imagine doing it for hour after hour, after hour?

TROLLING SPEED

The specifics of Homer LeBlanc's speed trolling tactics are amazingly basic and simple. Homer believed and so do I that the key to triggering strikes in warm water fishing conditions is maintaining speeds up to six miles per hour! To a guy who's primarily fishes walleye, salmon and other species, six miles per hour may sound unrealistics, but it works.

When the season opens in June and through August I keep my boat moving at this fast pace all the time. Not only does trolling fast trigger reactionary strikes, but it also allows me to cover an enormous amount of water during the course of eight or 10 hours of fishing.

When the water begins to cool in September, October and into November, trollers are forced to slow down to some degree. Cool water slows down the activity level of all fish and the musky is no exception. Still, in cool water trolling speeds around four miles per hour seem to

Trophy musky and northern pike are hard on fishing tackle. These lures have seen the enemy and lost.

produce the most strikes.

In the fall I also switch to larger baits. It's well documented that predator fish key on larger forage during the fall. Musky and other predators such as northern pike and walleye select larger forage during the fall period as a means of being more efficient in their feeding habits. keying on large prey allows them to feed less often, saving valuable energy that will be needed during the lean winter months and the rigors of the spring spawning periods.

MUSKY TROLLING LURES

A multitude of lures have been designed to catch musky. Despite what you might imagine a self proclaimed musky addict's tackle box looks like, I use a rather modest selection of baits including the Believer and Musky Stalker baits by Drifter Tackle. I like Believers in the eight inch and 10 inch models in both solid and jointed versions. The Musky Stalker is a smaller bait about six inches long that is used mostly during

189

the summer months.

I also have a lot of faith in a bait called the Terminator made by Esox Design. The model T-3 is my favorite. There are also many other excellent musky baits worth trying, but for my charter purposes these three basic lures fill a trolling niche nicely.

My color selection is also somewhat conservative. During the summer when the weather is mostly clear and bright, I prefer light colored and chrome lures such as mother of pearl, rainbow, light frog or blue and silver.

During the fall darker colors seem to produce better against the gray fall skies. My favorites are dark frog, yellow perch and the classic black and orange.

RODS/REELS/LINES

Chances are the rods you already own aren't going to be suitable for musky speed trolling tactics. I use three different rods types on my boat including a short three and a half footer that fishes straight out the back of the boat with the tip pointed down towards the water, a 10 foot Dipsy style rod that fishes out from the port and starboard sides and a six foot rod used on planer board lines.

My rods are all custom built, but with a little effort you can find suitable trolling rods at bait and tackle shops in the Lake St. Clair area. Anglers who live outside this region should consult rod manufactures to inquire about their salt water rod selection.

All my rods are made from fiberglass. Graphite rods are simply too fragile for the abuse this equipment receives. In other words, don't fool yourself into thinking your $100.00 graphite bucktail rod is okay for this type of fishing. Chances are your prized possession will be destroyed in short order.

For reels I'm sold on the standard Penn 309 levelwind reels. I also use Daiwa 47LC reels on my planer board rods. The line counter device on these reels is handy for monitoring trolling leads.

These reels are loaded with premium 40 pound test monofilament with a six foot leader of 100 pound test. The lures are connected to the leader using a stout cross loc style snap.

190

RIGGING TECHNIQUES

The rigging techniques used for musky speed trolling are somewhat unique. On planer board lines in-line style trolling weights ranging from one to four ounces are tied to the end of the 40 pound test main line. Next a six to eight foot leader of 100 pound test is added and the rig completed with a stout cross lok snap that accepts the bait.

In most trolling situations this rig receives a 30 to 40 foot trolling lead and is set out on a dual planer board running about 40 feet to the side of the boat. When musky trolling with boards it isn't necessary to set the boards out 75 or 100 feet to the side.

A single board line is run off each side of the boat. Each board line is attached to the tether line using an Off Shore Tackle OR-8 Heavy Tension release. This unique pinch pad line release features a double spring that provides the tension required to insure positive hooksets. If releases with less tension are used, many fish that strike are able to shake the bait free before being landed.

The Dipsy style rods receive the same rigging treatment as the board lines, but these rods are run perpendicular to the side of the boat with the tip pointed down towards the water. A rod 10 foot rod is set off each corner of the boat to help cover a little more water and spread out the lures into a loose school formation.

The stout three and a half footers that run straight off the back are equipped with much more weight. A full 16 ounce or 24 ounce lead ball is attached at the end of the main line with a heavy snap then a six foot leader of 100 pound test added.

The extra weight is required to keep these lines running right behind the motor prop. These lures are literally swimming in the prop wash and that's part of what makes them so effective.

Remember the attitude that musky live by. These lions of freshwater fishing aren't intimidated by fishing boats, but rather they thrive on the feeding opportunities provided when a boat passes through a school of baitfish. A Believer pulled in the prop wash does an excellent job of imitating a fish that's been injured or disorientated by the passing boat. Musky waste no time in taking advantage of this easy meal.

THE SIX LINE SET UP

Trolling with only six lines may seem odd to many trollers who are used to fishing eight, 10 or 12 lines. Much of the time planer lines are being trolled in areas that are littered with aquatic weeds anchored to the bottom or floating on the surface. The board lines must be cleared and checked constantly to make sure they aren't fouled with weeds, that's why I only run one board line on each side.

I'm a firm believer that six rods rigged correctly and fishing clean will out produce other boats fishing up to twice as many lines. It's just to hard to keep all the lines weed free when you start dealing with more than half a dozen lines.

WHERE THE ACTION TAKES PLACE

Good to excellent open water musky trolling opportunities occur throughout the deeper waters of Lake St. Clair. When you get into the shallow bays such as Mitchell's Bay, the primary predator switches from musky to the smaller northern pike.

I spend most of my time trolling in water from 12 to 15 feet deep. Early in the season before the weeds start to grow you can fish in water a little shallower.

Musky prefer the open waters of the lake, relating to a variety of features such as weed edges, bottom structure, channel edges, flowing water and debris on the bottom such as around the dumping grounds. Among these areas I have my most consistent success in places where two different colors of water come together.

Because Lake St. Clair has a major river flowing in (St. Clair River) and a major flow going out (Detroit River) there's always a movement of water passing through the lake. The lake also receives a considerable amount of boat traffic that stirs up the water and adds to the movement of water colors.

CASHING IN ON NORTHERN PIKE

My charter business focuses strictly on musky. However, I usually take three or four dozen trophy size northern pike a year as a bonus to my musky fishing efforts. Trolling tactics for musky can be equally effective on pike so long as some minor modifications are made.

First off, since northern pike are smaller fish on the average than musky, I'd downsize my lures to specifically target pike. Many of the classic lures used for musky will work on pike, plus a wealth of other body baits such as the Storm Shallow Mac, Rebel Minnow, Bomber, A.C. Plug and Super Shad Rap are good choices.

Also, pike are more likely to end up in deep water than musky. In many waters northerns suspend in the water column over deep water mud flats. Pike living in these areas feed on suspended forages such as smelt, ciscoes, alewives or shad and have no reason to come near a weed bed all summer long.

To fish these deep water areas I'd want a few diving cranks that are capable of fishing from 10 to 30 feet below the surface. A few baits that come to mind include the Storm Little and Big Mac, Deep Diving ThunderStick and Magnum Wiggle Wart, plus the Bomber 26A, Luhr Jensen Powerdive Minnow, Mann's Stretch 20 and 25 and Cotton Cordell's Magnum Wally Diver. The obvious way to fish these lures is with planer boards.

I'd also drop my trolling speed down considerably when targeting northern pike. Trolling speeds ranging from three to four miles per hour are ideal for northerns.

If I found myself fishing more traditional pike water such as weed edges or over the tops of weed beds, I'd stick with shallow diving lures and the six rod system described for musky speed trolling.

Trolling for northern pike also brings up another question. Will the tactics I use to catch musky on Lake St. Clair work elsewhere? The answer is yes. A musky acts like a musky no matter where he lives. Speed trolling is one of the most effective ways of finding and catching these popular trophies.

However, there's also some bad news to report. On many waters especially in Northern Wisconsin, trolling is not allowed for musky fishing. Fisheries managers fear that the delicate population of fish in many of these waters would be seriously damaged if trolling tactics were allowed. Before testing out these tactics, check with your local game and fish department about special regulations against musky trolling in certain waters.

Ironically, it wouldn't matter how you choose to catch musky if more anglers would simply release their fish to fight again. With the technology

Big northern pike are often found in open water. This trophy was taken while trolling crankbaits in Little Bay de Noc.

we have today to produce excellent replica fish mounts, there's no reason to ever kill a trophy class musky.

I believe that musky are more valuable in the water than they are hanging on the wall. After all, it's the mysteriousness of big fish that attracts anglers to musky fishing. The dream of someday hooking into a 30, 40 or 50 pound musky is what keeps this unique breed of fisherman coming back for more.

The same could be said of all trophy class fish. The trolling tactics detailed in this book will make anyone a more efficient and successful angler. With this newly acquired skill comes the responsibility of knowing when to say enough.

I sincerely hope that all who read this book will abide by a simple code of ethics. Limit your kill instead of killing your limit.

Don Miller is a charter captain, fishing educator and musky trolling addict.

Book Ordering Information

PRECISION TROLLING: By Mark Romanack and Dr. Steven Holt. The trollers bible, this flip-chart style guide answers the question of how deep does it dive. Depth diving data is provided for over 120 crankbaits, diving planers, lead core line, snap weights and more. Used by thousands of serious trollers, copies are available for $19.95 plus $4.50 shipping and handling.

FIVE ROADS TO WALLEYE: By Mark Romanack. This 200 page paperback book explores the five common lure groups used to catch walleye including jigs, live bait rigs, spoons, crankbaits and floats. Each chapter is dedicated to a different fish catching technique. Copies are $14.95 plus $3.50 shipping.

ADVANCED WALLEYE STRATEGIES: By Mark Romanack. This beautiful hard bound book is a comprehensive guide to walleye fishing. Over 250 pages of text, 75 photographs and illustrations are used to help readers understand the finer points of walleye fishing. Copies are $19.95, plus $3.50 shipping.

ORDERING INFORMATION

Books are available from Book Central, PO Box 317, Tustin, MI, 49688. Checks, money orders, Visa, Discover and MasterCard are accepted. Call 1-616-829-5171 for credit card orders. Canadian orders please add $5.00 shipping and handling.